D1466974

HUNTING SECRETS
OF THE EXPERTS

BOOKS BY VLAD EVANOFF

HUNTING SECRETS OF THE EXPERTS

THE FRESH-WATER FISHERMAN'S BIBLE

FISHING SECRETS OF THE EXPERTS

HOW TO FISH IN SALT WATER

COMPLETE GUIDE TO FISHING

MODERN FISHING TACKLE

HOW TO MAKE FISHING LURES

NATURAL BAITS FOR FISHERMEN

SPIN FISHING

NATURAL SALT WATER FISHING BAITS

SURF FISHING

HUNTING SECRETS
OF THE EXPERTS

Edited by Vlad Evanoff

Drawings by the Editor

DOUBLEDAY & COMPANY, INC.
GARDEN CITY, NEW YORK

LIBRARY OF CONGRESS CATALOG CARD NUMBER 64–19061
COPYRIGHT © 1964 BY DOUBLEDAY & COMPANY, INC.
ALL RIGHTS RESERVED
PRINTED IN THE UNITED STATES OF AMERICA

ACKNOWLEDGMENTS

The editor wishes to thank the following for supplying photos which were used in the book: The Canadian Government Travel Bureau; Canadian Pacific Railway; Maine Department of Economic Development; South Dakota Department of Game, Fish and Parks; Tennessee Game and Fish Commission and the U. S. Fish and Wildlife Service. Photographs otherwise unidentified are from the authors of the various chapters.

FOREWORD

WHEN an earlier book called *Fishing Secrets of the Experts* came out I gave a copy to a friend of mine who is both an angler and a hunter. He looked the book over and said that it was a good idea and that a similar book should be published dealing with hunting. I agreed with him that his suggestion had merit and proposed the idea to the publishers of the fishing book. The editor at Doubleday, Ferris Mack, who handles outdoor books, was interested in such a hunting compilation but wanted to wait to see how the fishing book fared.

The fishing book soon proved to be very popular with the nation's anglers. So in due time a contract was signed giving me the green light for the hunting book. Because of the success of the earlier book I decided to follow the same format and procedure used in the fishing book. That is, to choose the men best qualified to write about hunting a specific kind of game. So, as for the fishing book, some of the top men in the country were approached. Some of these hunters have national reputations, and are well-known because of their books or magazine articles. Others have more limited reputations within their own areas but are no less expert in their specialties.

One thing all these hunters have in common is the skill and know-how required to a bag a certain kind of game. Many of them have spent a lifetime studying and seeking a certain species. All of them have spent many years hunting the species they write about in these pages. Roger Latham, who writes about wild turkeys, is considered an authority on this elusive and exciting bird. Frank C. Hibben, who writes about black bears, once spent eight months hunting black bears and grizzlies to obtain information for a book. Jimmy Robinson spends at least two months a year shooting ducks and geese in Canada. Bert

Popowski is probably the country's top expert on crow hunting. You'll find all these hunters in this book and many others who are equally qualified experts.

Besides being skilled hunters, these contributors to the book are also good writers. After all, their know-how isn't of much use to another hunter unless it can be passed on simply and clearly. The advice and guidance in this book can be read, understood —and enjoyed—by anyone interested in hunting. You'll find many "how-to-do-it" tips about hunting methods and techniques which have been acquired by countless years, days, and hours spent in the field. The man (or woman) who reads this volume will become a better hunter if he uses some of the tips, hints, and "secrets" recommended by these experts.

VLAD EVANOFF

CONTENTS

ILLUSTRATIONS

HUNTING SECRETS
OF THE EXPERTS

Spot nuzzles the hide of a fox shot after a long, hard chase. Ted Janes, author of this chapter, is on the left. His hunting companion is Dick Fowler.

Chapter One

OUTWITTING THE FOX
by TED JANES

TED JANES has always been connected with the outdoor publishing field as an editorial worker or free-lance writer. He has contributed hundreds of stories and articles to the outdoor magazines and has had nine books published on hunting, fishing, camping, boating, and related fields. At the present time he is Eastern Field Editor of *Outdoor Life* magazine, a job which takes him on hunting and fishing assignments from Maine to West Virginia. When he is not on these trips he spends his time hunting and fishing around his home in Westfield, Massachusetts.

THE guile of Reynard the fox is legendary and most of the legends are true, or, at least, are based upon fact. And let us make clear at the outset that we are talking now about the red fox and not the gray, which is only a dim-witted, tree-climbing, quick-to-hole-up imitation of his rufous cousin. Red foxes often run among sheep or cattle to obliterate their scent, though it is doubtful if they ever ride on these animals as legend asserts. For the same reason, they follow stone walls and shallow streams and at times will even swim if need be.

Foxes are also said to relieve one another when hard-pressed by the hounds. A fresh fox is supposed to take the place of its tiring partner by intercepting the dogs, but this, I think is a sort of half-truth. A fox will, upon occasion, throw the hounds onto the trail of another fox, but without the knowledge or consent of the latter. It seems to be, rather, a sort of vulpine practical joke.

Another half-truth is the commonly held belief that foxes deliberately lure dogs to destruction ahead of speeding trains. It probably happens occasionally, but, if so, it is doubtless due to coincidence. Foxes do, however, frequently follow railroad tracks for the same reason that they follow stone walls—because the steel rails and trap-rock ballast soon vitiate their scent. They have learned, too, that fumes from gasoline and hot rubber have the same effect and many a modern fox hunt has ended in defeat at the edge of a busy highway.

Faced with this sort of artful dodging, it might seem to be a practical impossibility to tack Reynard's pelt to the wall, but, fortunately, there are ways to outwit him. Even when you fail, which is frequently, the thrill of hunting him invariably affords memorable days afield.

The traditional method of outwitting foxes, of course, is by trailing them with hounds. In the South, this often means a pack of hounds followed by pink-coated riders mounted on timber-topping horses. Or it may be a small coterie of native sons sprawled around a mountain campfire, listening to good hound music welling beneath the stars. In both these types of hunting, it is the chase alone that matters, and there is no thought of killing the fox unless perchance the job is done by the dogs themselves, a most remote possibility in the case of the resourceful red fox.

In the North the trailing is done by one or two hounds, rangy and gaunt from hard running, dogs which can follow the quarry hour after hour over hilltop pastures, through swamps and uplands until at last it comes within range of the hunter concealed in a juniper thicket or crouched behind a tumble-down stone wall. It is this combination of good dogs and of hunters who know where to take up their stands that brings this kind of fox hunt to a successful conclusion.

As a first step in hunting with hounds, it is important to realize that foxes in their travels follow runways established by their early ancestors and slavishly adhered to by succeeding generations up to the present. Foxes are still being shot today in my native Berkshire Hills in exactly the same places where their forebears met their doom a century, a half-century, or a decade ago.

Therefore, it will be seen that a knowledge of these invisible paths is a prime requisite for successful fox hunting and has a

In the North foxes are hunted with one or two hounds—rangy, hard-hunting dogs. These dogs are Spot and Diver, two typical foxhounds.

great deal to do with ultimately outwitting the quarry. This knowledge is gained either by trial and error, or preferably, from some veteran fox hunter, a man like old Ben Grant who flourished in our town when the century was somewhat younger.

Ben could stand on a pasture hill with the wind-blown tumult of the chase in his ears and tell you exactly what the fox was doing.

"He's swingin' behind Parson's Hill," he'd say, cocking his head to one side. "He tried to fool the dogs at the brook, but they've picked him up again . . . Now he's heading for the top of Wolf Hill."

Having ascertained the general trend of the situation, he'd place himself and his companions in strategic places—at barways, beside ledges, and on wood roads—along the route he knew the fox would take. Sooner or later someone would usually have a shot at the streaking red target.

This, in its simplest form, is the theory of hunting foxes with dogs, but, unfortunately—or fortunately for the fox—within this framework anything can happen and usually does. For these runways are not isolated trails circling the hills, but consist rather of a network of invisible paths which branch and fork and overlap from one fox range to another across the countryside. Over them the hounded fox races like a runaway locomotive over open switches. He may head for Wolf Hill, only to veer off on a side track and lead the dogs four or five miles in the op- posite direction. And he may never return to his starting point, for, contrary to general belief, foxes do not usually circle, es- pecially today's canny breed.

Even when you've guessed right as to his route, a smart old red will frequently cross you up, hopelessly confusing the follow- ing dogs or managing to sneak past your stand unseen. And, finally, a bounding fox, streaking past an opening in the trees is not the easiest target to hit, even when the fleeting opportunity offers. Perhaps the best way to make clear some of the difficulties of outwitting red Reynard would be to describe one or two typical encounters chosen at random from my own fox-hunting experience.

There was the old dog fox—Big Red, we called him—that

hung out in Timber Swamp. We could pick him up there most any morning, and sometimes I think he came there hoping for a run. I had a pair of Walkers named Ranger and Bell, and in time they came to look upon Big Red as their personal enemy Number 1. Day after day, they'd pick up his trail and go racket-ing off on a smoking scent.

Invariably the chase led off to the rugged slopes of Grindstone Mountain, and from our stands we'd hear the music swelling and fading around its wooded sides. But no one ever got a shot at the red phantom, although one time Charlie Drake caught a glimpse of him scrambling his tracks out of gun range in a freshly manured field. And inevitably the trail would end abruptly at the edge of a high-banked brook that ran along a railroad embankment. We'd hear the swelling chorus change to uncertain mutterings as the baffled dogs feathered along its wind-ing course. We posted hunters beside the brook and along the tracks, because foxes will often follow cold iron, but this fox had a better scheme than that.

We learned what it was when the first snowstorm of winter covered the frozen brook. I was below the embankment that day as the rioting chase came near, and I climbed to the tracks just in time to see the dogs burst from the woods. This time they never faltered as they followed hot scent along the frozen, snowy channel of the brook to where it ran through a culvert under the embankment. Up to now the water had covered Big Red's trail, but today the snow betrayed him. At full tilt Ranger hurled him-self into the culvert only to become tightly wedged in its dark interior. It took the combined efforts of three hunters to pry him loose, and only later did someone think to look on the far side of the culvert through which Big Red had long since made his exit, laughing.

There was another fox that led Dick Fowler and me a merry chase that began in Lyman's pasture and ended on Pomeroy Mountain seven miles away and nine hours later. We loosed Dick's dogs, Blackie and Spot, at the edge of the juniper-grown pasture and watched them zigzag among the low evergreens, vacuuming the frozen ground for a wisp of scent. Soon they had disappeared from sight, leaving us to the winter silence. The

23

sibilant lisping of chickadees sounded from nearby thickets and from the woods beyond came the hollow ring of an ax. And then suddenly a mournful, questing cry rose uncertainly upon the breeze.

"That's Blackie!" Dick said.

The high-pitched voice sounded again, and a moment later Spot's deep baritone chimed in. Now the two voices rose in a rhythmic, chopping cadence that made my backbone twang. As the riotous music faded beyond the ridge, Dick cradled his 12-gauge autoloader across his elbow.

"He's taking them over Bungy," he said, "and we'd better make tracks for Searles's mowing."

We made tracks, quite a lot of them, and came at last to a wide meadow, only to find that we were too late. The chase had passed by and we could hear the dogs' ringing duet drifting back from the ridge as they moved toward Deer Mountain. We raced up its wooded slopes to take our positions on a ledge overlooking the valley. The dogs' challenging voices belled from a spur ahead of us and then suddenly fell away to silence. Presently we saw them feathering up the ravine. Finally they found the trail again, but it led straight away from us, and we had to move to another stand.

I took a position beside a big pine high on the mountainside while Dick sought a favorite spot among the hemlocks. From my stand I could hear the dogs' bawling chant moving in from the west. Then it faded again far to the south. For a few minutes more I stood catching my breath and huddling deeper into my coat, stamping numb feet on the frozen ground. Then Dick appeared.

"They've led away for Flat Hill," he said. "No use to stay here any longer. Come on."

We clambered from the steep slope, crossed the narrow valley and circled the wooded side of Flat Hill. From a stand beside a big pine on a high ridge where I could look down upon wide fields, frozen brown earth and faded pastures alternating in a patchwork-quilt effect. The only sounds now were the cawing of crows above the pines and the far off whine of a portable sawmill. I ate a half-frozen sandwich and smoked my pipe. I looked to the number 4 shells nestled in the chambers of my 16-gauge over-and-under. I kicked booted feet against the pine-tree trunk and waited, listening, watching, cold.

Then, faint in the distance, I heard the dogs—Blackie's yelping falsetto and Spot's clamorous baritone—driving along Moose Brook. Suddenly, a flicker of motion at the edge of the woods caught my eye and there was the fox drifting like a tawny shadow across the field, head outstretched, plume trailing away behind his graceful, bounding form. I could feel my pulses thud as I watched him leap to the top of a stone wall which separated pasture from mowing. There he paused, glancing back at the dogs.

The breeze ruffled the fur on his back, and the sunlight burnished it to rich copper tones. He trotted along the wall, dropped down on the far side, leaped up again, and continued on. At its end he sprang with a great bound into the field, and then as I watched, fascinated, he ran back and forth several times before bounding again to the wall. He stood there for a second glancing at the woods. Then, as if satisfied, he turned and trotted toward me.

He was less than a hundred yards away—eighty—seventy—I snicked off the safety and cautiously raised my gun. And at the same instant the fox suddenly whirled and sped away for the opposite woods, just as the dogs broke from cover. Whether he had heard the faint click of the safety or had winded me I'll never know, but he was gone like a rufous phantom, and all our scheming and hard work so far had gone for nought. At least I was able to put the baffled hounds on the trail again, and they took after the fleeting fox with all the stops out while Dick and I had a hurried conference on the mountainside.

"What do we do now?" I asked, and Dick shrugged.

"Keep on chasing," he replied. "One thing is for sure. Blackie and Spot will never quit while they can stand up." He listened for a moment to the fading baying of the dogs. "He's going toward Pomeroy," he said. "Maybe we can head him off at the ledges."

We hurried back to the car on aching legs and drove furiously up Crooked Ledge Road, jolting over rocks and frozen ruts. At the top of the knoll we could hear the dogs' rhythmic chop floating down from Parson's Hill.

"He's in the swamp," Dick said. "We'll never make it to the ledges. Let's try the pasture on Pomeroy."

Neither one of us talked much as we waded through laurel swamps up the mountainside. We were both too tired for one thing, and for another we were feeling discouraged. We'd been chasing that fox since morning, and now blue shadows were beginning to slant across the fields. Soon the game would have to be called on account of darkness. In the gathering dusk we reached the pasture and stood catching our breath at its edge.

"You stand at the corner," Dick said, "and I'll go up to the barway."

I had hardly taken my stand before I heard the dogs' voices rising and falling against the forest sounds like a thread of melody woven into a symphony. Closer and closer they came and now their ringing aria broke in waves against the hills and washed down into the valley. Driving hard, the chase swept along the side of Pomeroy Mountain and burst in clamorous fury around its wooded slopes. A second later the fox burst from a patch of juniper, clearing the pasture fence in a graceful bound. My first shot showered dirt behind him but at the second he somersaulted and lay kicking feebly as the dogs broke out of the woods.

These two typical examples, I think, will show some of the problems one almost always encounters in attempting to outwit the sly red fox. It takes a thorough knowledge of the countryside and especially of the location of the maze of fox runs through it. It takes hard-driving dogs, patience, stamina, and, in the end, a sizable chunk of luck.

So much for trailing the fox with hounds. There is another hunting method which is even more difficult, but which, perhaps for that very reason, affords even greater satisfactions. This is the sport of stalking foxes, a game in which the hunter matches wits with his quarry without benefit of dogs. Successful stalking requires a complete understanding of fox nature and habits, a superior brand of woodsmanship, and, again, a dollop of luck.

Success in stalking is best achieved by taking advantage of

the fox's routine, for like all animals, Reynard is a creature of habit. Much of his hunting is done at night or in the early morning for his favorite delicacies—mice, rabbits, birds, frogs, beetles, and, if opportunity offers, plump chickens from the farmer's poultry house. Having filled his stomach, he seeks out some favorite spot where he can lie concealed while he naps and digests his dinner.

This favored location is almost always at or near the top of a knoll which affords a good view of the countryside, and it may consist of a rocky ledge, a log, or a stump. Whichever it is, when he lies down with his bushy tail curled like a warm blanket over his nose and pads, he has an amazing ability to blend with his surroundings and become to all intents and purposes a rust-colored rock, a burl on a log, or a part of a tree stump. It is only when one is able to look at him closely that his presence is betrayed by the breeze ruffling his fur. For this reason, a pair of 7- or 8-power binoculars is an important item of equipment for the fox hunter.

Foxes are apt to return each day to the same spot unless they are disturbed, so a knowledge of these locations is of great importance. The best way to carry on this hunting is to lie in wait some distance away with a scope-sighted rifle. If you don't know the location of these favored lying-up spots, you can often find them after the snows have come.

Get out at dawn after a light snowfall and you can read on nature's clean white page a revealing autobiography of Reynard. Here are his small, round prints, set daintily one before the other in a manner which the awkward dog could never hope to emulate. They lead out of a laurel tangle to follow along a muted winter brook. A hundred yards farther on there is a slight depression where the fox has crouched, belly to the snow. Now the tracks show in curved sets of four with wide spaces in between as the fox bounds after his prey, and a short distance away a few scraps of fur and bone and a crimson spot on the snow mark the successful culmination of Reynard's search for his dinner.

Now the tracks move on along the brook, and when they veer up into the ledges it is best to leave them and circle slowly and

Foxes can be followed after a snowfall. A walking or trotting fox leaves tracks almost in line. A dog's tracks are more staggered.

cautiously, keeping a sharp watch on the ground ahead. Give special attention to stumps, boulders, and logs, and hold your gun ready, for at any second the fox may spring from such a spot. Or it may be that he will hear you and all you will find are his tracks bounding away from a windswept ridge.

If the fox has a weakness, it is for mice, and this fact, too, can be used to advantage in hunting him. Not many men, though, are as expert in its exploitation as was Joe Graham, who showed me how it is done. I went with Joe to a hillside mowing frequented by foxes one winter morning when hard-polished stars still studded the sky.

"There's been foxes mousing in this field," Joe whispered as we moved cautiously along its edge. "We might do some business here—if we're lucky."

Crouched behind a stone wall we waited, cramped and cold, while a gray light broke in the east. I had come along, half incredulous, to see the old hunter perform the feat he had often told me about, but after an hour's vigil in the winter cold I was ready to call it quits. Then suddenly Joe nudged me, and, fol-

28

lowing his glance, I saw a fox trotting across a corner of the mowing. As I watched, he paused, listening. Then, gathering his muscles, he sprang, burying his face in the snow in his efforts to capture a field mouse scurrying along its white-walled tunnel. Apparently he missed, for he shook the snow from his muzzle and again stood listening. While he did so, Joe Graham jerked off his mitten and, placing the back of his hand to his lips, emitted a high-pitched squeak.

Instantly the fox's head came up, ears erect, sharp snout turned inquiringly toward us. Then, to my amazement, he began moving slowly in our direction. Sixty yards away he paused again, head cocked to one side like a dog. Once again Joe put his hand to his lips and squeaked softly. The fox stole forward once more, and I could feel Joe stir beside me. When the fox was only thirty yards away and still coming toward us, Joe snicked off the safety of his 12-gauge double and rose to his feet. The fox whirled in a red blur but before he had taken two bounds, a blast of chilled 4s sent him sprawling end-over-end in the snow.

"A fox just naturally can't resist a chance at a mouse," Joe said as he clambered over the wall to pick up his prize.

Not everyone can make this realistic mouse squeak, which is done by kissing the back of one's hand, but, fortunately, there are on the market today predator calls with which anyone can achieve a convincing imitation of a mouse's squeak. It is incredible, too, how far away a fox can hear this sound, and if you are well hidden and the breeze is blowing toward you, nine times out of ten, the fox will come to your call, for, as old Joe Graham said, red Reynard is a patsy for a mouse.

For most kinds of fox hunting a shotgun is better than a rifle, the one exception, as we have said, being long-range shooting with a telescope sight. Any size shot from number 2 to number 4 is adequate, and I have killed a fox with number 6 shot, for, again contrary to popular opinion, the fox is a small animal, scarcely larger than a good-sized cat. When his thick coat is removed, the carcass is surprisingly tiny. For most occasions, I think number 4s are about ideal.

However you hunt him, with bugling hounds, crouched patiently behind a stone wall, or following his roving tracks through the snowy woods, it takes plenty of experience, knowledge, skill, and, as we have said, luck, to outwit Reynard. But whether you win or lose, hunting him is a fascinating sport that never loses its zest, for, always, the red fox does the unexpected.

Chapter Two

COTTONTAIL-RABBIT HUNTING
by TOM MCNALLY

TOM MCNALLY is a newspaperman and writer who spends all his time hunting or fishing and writing about it. He is one of the country's most prolific writers with by-lines in the top outdoor magazines month after month. He also writes hunting and fishing guides and booklets and edits the *Fishermen's Digest.* At the present time he is outdoor editor of the Chicago *Tribune,* where his column is popular with many hunters and anglers. How he ever gets any writing done is a mystery because he spends much of his time traveling all over the country and to many parts of the world gathering material for his stories.

O F ALL North American game, none is more avidly sought —and found—than the cottontail rabbit. Brer Cottontail lives— and thrives—in every state. He is here, and there, and over there, too; and probably even in the flower garden in your backyard.

The lowly bunny furnishes more hunting for more hunters than all other game combined. Nearly every adult sportsman "cut his hunter's teeth" as a boy out chasing cottontails. An individual adult sportsman today might get his "kicks" by busting buffalo or executing elephants; but chances are the first game he tumbled was an inoffensive rabbit.

Cottontails are really important in some places. They are especially abundant in the grain fields of the Midwest. Missouri, Illinois, South Dakota, Nebraska, Arkansas, and Oklahoma are literally infested with rabbits. Missouri and Illinois especially have large cottontail populations. In Missouri rabbits probably outnumber people; hunters there annually bag in excess of six million rabbits. The take in Illinois is nearly as great, running to around five million.

In some other states, particularly those that are thickly

31

Tom McNally.

wooded, it would be easier to find a prize white-tailed deer than a healthy rabbit. The northern parts of Maine, Wisconsin, Minnesota, and Michigan, for example, are not exactly notable rabbit-hunting areas. But even in such places, always—year after year—there are *some* rabbits.

No expensive paraphernalia is required for rabbit hunting. Some old but tough clothes, a gun, some shells—that's all that is basically needed to "do in" a bundle of rabbits. But the devoted rabbit hunter, of course, is happier with better equipment. Some addicted rabbit hunters, in fact, are just as nattily attired and as expensively gunned as a buckboard-riding quail hunter working the cotton-patch edges on a Georgia plantation. The major difference between them might be the etching on their guns; the Georgian's is carved to quail, the rabbit hunter's to bunnies.

Considering weapons first, cottontails are hunted with everything from slingshots to souped-up rifles. But the best weapon, of course, is a shotgun. A variety of shotguns are suitable for hunting rabbits. Much depends on the hunter's preference, whether or not hounds are used, the kind of cover hunted, and the sportsman's shooting ability. Most popular rabbit guns are 20, 16, and 12 gauge. In experienced and straight-shooting hands, there's nothing wrong with 28- and .410-gauge shotguns.

If most of your hunting is done in open country and shots are at long range, a 12 gauge with full choke will probably serve you best. A full choke keeps the shot load together for a greater distance, thus providing a tighter pellet pattern at thirty-five yards and beyond. If your rabbit hunting is varied—sometimes in heavy cover, sometimes in the open—use a 12-gauge modified choke. Modified is the best all-around bore. It gives a reasonably "open" pattern at close range; a fairly "tight" and quite effective pattern to forty yards.

For rabbit hunting in thick cover, where shots at close range are the rule and fast gun-handling is important, a 20 gauge with modified choke is excellent. (A 16 gauge, in measured performance, differs little from a 12.)

Most popular shot size for rabbits is No. 6, high-power. Actually, rabbits are not tenacious, and under many conditions much lighter loads such as low-power 9s are desirable.

33

The lowly bunny furnishes more hunting for more hunters than all other game combined. He's not only popular with most kids but also with millions of adult hunters seeking sport and good eating.

As in hunting all other kinds of game, it's a matter of personal preference whether the rabbit gun is an automatic, pump repeater, double-barrel, over-and-under, or single shot. Least desirable is the single shot, since second shots often are needed. It's not normally possible, or practical, to get a third shot—provided by most automatic and pump guns—at fast-moving rabbits.

Automatics, double-barrels, over-unders are the heaviest shotguns, in that order. Automatics, pumps, over-unders, and single barrels give single-barrel sighting which many hunters consider desirable. They feel that a single-barrel shotgun is more easily and quickly pointed than a double or over-under, even though the latter provides single-plane sighting.

The scatterpiece I tote into the bunny patches is a lightweight 20-gauge pump. Barrel length is 26 inches, and choke modified. With the comparatively short barrel and a weight of 6¼ pounds, the gun handles very fast and can be lugged all day without fatigue.

In most states rabbit season opens in early fall and continues through the winter; thus both light and heavy hunting clothes are needed. Most important are the trousers; both the light and heavy ones should be faced with a tough material to make them brierproof. Heavy canvas facing is preferred to leather; leather repels briers best, but it is heavy and a real drudge to the hunter when it's wet. In rabbit hunting it is often necessary to get right into briers and kick around, otherwise hidden rabbits may not move out.

Footwear is also important, since rabbit hunters usually do considerable hiking. A durable but light pair of rubber-bottomed shoepacks are ideal, and in dry weather a pair of 10- or 12-inch-high bird-shooter boots are fine. Bird and pac boots will do for nearly all rabbit hunting, but in late winter when snows are piled high and the temperature low you may want a pair of all-rubber insulated boots. These thermo boots will keep your feet warm and dry in the wettest, coldest weather. The rabbit hunter who does much walking should wear a thin pair of nylon or silk hose, and a pair of warm, soft, woolen socks over them.

An ordinary hunting coat made of tough cotton drill or other

35

suitable material will do nicely for hunting rabbits. It should be waterproof, or at least water repellent. It should have ample pockets, including a large game pocket (also good for carrying lunch), and be reasonably lightweight. Many an aching back, following a day's hunt, can be attributed to a hunting coat that was unnecessarily heavy.

A visored leather, corduroy, or cotton drill cap is not necessary, but it is helpful. It can keep rain or snow from your face and shield your eyes from the glare of the sun just at that crucial moment when a rabbit bursts from cover.

The cottontail feeds and romances by night, when it wanders aimlessly, but rabbits habitually use particular trails when in their favorite cover. When jumped by hunters or hounds, a rabbit may circle endlessly, but soon as possible it will get on one of its trails—so find a spot where a couple of bunny "roads" converge and stay there until your dogs run the rabbit your way.

Generally speaking, cottontails rely on two stratagems for survival: absolute immobility and headlong flight. A hunter walking too fast will bypass many a squatting bunny, so work cover slowly and carefully. It must be remembered that rabbits are nocturnal. They are normally really active only at night. During the day, they "bed" in nests they form in heavy grass, leaves, broom sage, weeds, honeysuckle, briers, and so on. As a rule a man or dog must almost step on rabbits hidden in their beds before the rabbit will "jump," that is, show himself by running off. Frequently you may walk within a yard or two of a sulking rabbit, and Brer Bunny won't move. You may go right on by without ever knowing how close you'd come to the makings for rabbit potpie. When in good cover where you are sure rabbits should be, pause frequently. Walk a few yards and stop—walk a few more—and stop. If a rabbit is near, he'll grow nervous each time you halt, thinking he's discovered, and if he's a normal cottontail he won't be able to stand the suspense and will take off in high gear. Experienced rabbit hunters especially stop when near brush heaps, small clumps of briers, and wood piles —all good places for rabbits to bed.

Always work lightly cover slowly and carefully. The hunter who blunders his way along, trying to cover many miles quickly

A rabbit hunter should move slowly and stop every few yards. This makes a rabbit nervous, and he will take off.

instead of limited cover thoroughly, is not likely to jump many rabbits.

When a rabbit is jumped in dense cover, pick a spot ahead of the bunny—where you next expect the rabbit to be—and let go with your shotgun at the right moment. Often your shot charge will penetrate the brush barrier, and you'll collect your rabbit. Never, of course, shoot into brush that is high or so dense that you do not know what lies beyond. By shooting into brush, I mean those times when a trotting cottontail—one you already are tracing with your gun—ducks behind or through limited broom sage or such other low cover. You can shoot at such a rabbit and likely get him without endangering any companions or someone's prized beagle that might be trailing the rabbit. Hunting safety always is any hunter's first responsibility!

Cottontails are found in a wide variety of cover types. But cornfields, "brushy" fences, hedgerows, stone walls, honeysuckle

37

and brier patches, swamps and swales, sassafras thickets, and some open fields are all good places to search for rabbits.

"Walking 'em up," a method whereby several hunters form a line and stroll slowly through likely cover, is the most common system of hunting rabbits. This technique is ideal for group hunts, but it's usually wise, for safety reasons, not to hunt in parties of more than four. A rabbit may jump just in front of a line of hunters, and probably he'll run straight away or quarter a bit left or right. But sometimes the rabbits, confused, swing around and run right through the hunter's line. At such a moment the inexperienced and easily excited gunner may swing with his shotgun and endanger a companion.

When hunting near very heavy, impenetrable cover, stand ready with your shotgun and try tossing heavy stones or limbs into the cover. Sometimes this will spook a hidden rabbit and provide you with a shot.

Lone hunters utilize the "walk up" method, simply strolling slowly through likely cover, poking here and there where cover is thickest, and are often very successful in routing several rabbits. But it's better to hunt rabbits—assuming no dogs are involved—with a companion or two. When there's more than one hunter, a rabbit-hunting "team" evolves. In heavily matted undergrowth a rabbit will often skulk along, nosing his way slowly and sneakily through the brush. A lone hunter may not detect such a pussyfooting bunny. But if there are two hunters or more divided on either side of such cover, one or the other of the sportsmen is likely to see the rabbit and . . . *boom!*

Sneaking, incidentally, is especially common among swamp rabbits and those living in heavy grass swales.

During severe storms or periods of bad weather, rabbits go underground, seeking shelter in woodchuck holes, in hollow tree roots, beneath overhanging banks and grass clumps. They emerge from such places when the weather clears, and this is one of the best times to hunt rabbits, just after severe storms.

Like most animals, rabbits enjoy their comfort. To them, comfort is food and snug shelter. The best areas for rabbit hunting offer both. A cornfield, soybean patch, clover planting, or some other farm-crop field, surrounded by excellent cover such as

Cottontail rabbits are apt to be found almost anywhere, but they are most plentiful in cornfields, brushy fences, hedgerows, along stone walls, in honeysuckle and brier patches, and in sassafras thickets.

thick honeysuckle fencing, is certain to have a fair contingent of cottontails. Rabbits are communal critters, however. At times, both cover and food are present in a given area, yet there will be no rabbits. Only another rabbit knows why this is so.

Very often hunters may work an entire cornfield, one surrounded by briers or honeysuckle, and jump not a rabbit until, finally, in one distant corner of the field many rabbits suddenly are arunning.

Once, hunting near Momence, Illinois, Leo Pachner and I had only so-so hunting, getting three or four rabbits a day. Then, in the same area we had been hunting, we stumbled upon a forty-acre field of asparagus. For the next two days we hunted only the "asparagus patch." It seemed every rabbit in the county had settled in that one small field.

The peak of rabbit hunting comes when a brace or more of beagle hounds is used. The dogs often rout rabbits from their beds, and the dogs take off—baying musically—on the trail of a rabbit they've disturbed. Good beagles seldom lose a cottontail, unless the rabbit makes it to a woodchuck hole or other cover where the dogs can't follow. Normally quality beagles run a rabbit consistently but slowly until a hunter's shot tumbles it. Frequently such rabbit-dog chases last for hours.

In most states it is permissible to track rabbits following fresh snowfall. In states where this is legal, tracking rabbits can be fine sport. Even the youngsters enjoy going along on rabbit-tracking expeditions. It's a good way to get children to digest some nature lore, because many interesting things can be pointed out to them in the course of sleuthing along a bunny's trail.

Tracks that rabbits make at night may be intricate, but a careful hunter can work them out. This method of rabbit hunting is every bit as sporty as other methods, and, if you want to make it really tough for yourself, use a bow and arrow.

Rabbit hunting is not a "sissy" sport. Even those hunters who work with dogs must usually cover long and arduous miles in the course of a day at chasing cottontails. They hike the sloughs and the swales, trudge the draws and the ravines, pound the briers and the thistles, and break through the corn and the honeysuckle. It can be strenuous, back-busting, footsore work when rabbits are hunted hard.

Many rabbit hunters sometimes "give out." But rabbits, of course, never do.

Cottontail-
Rabbit Hunting

42   Russell Tinsley.

Chapter Three

SHOOTING JACK RABBITS

by RUSSELL TINSLEY

RUSSELL TINSLEY lives in Austin, Texas, where he writes an outdoor column for the *American-Statesman*. He's an avid hunter and angler, traveling to various parts of Texas, neighboring states, and Mexico for his sport and to gather material for his articles. In addition to his newspaper column he also writes many stories for outdoor, gun, and fishing magazines. Having hunted jack rabbits since he was a boy in Texas, where he was born and raised, he knows a lot about these long-eared critters.

WINSTON lowered his binoculars. "How far is that jack rabbit?" I asked in an urgent whisper.

He shaded his eyes against the low-hanging afternoon sun. "Oh, somewhere in the vicinity of 280 yards."

Steadying the .222 Remington rifle across my knees, I located the long-eared critter in the 6-power scope sight. It was sitting upright in the heart of a long, open, grassy clearing in northern Mexico, near the hamlet of San Fernando on the east coast. From the small knoll where Winston and I were sitting, I'd be shooting slightly down at it, but not enough to make any discernible difference in bullet placement. Anyway, the tendency when shooting down on your target is to overshoot, which was all right, since the 50-grain bullet would drop somewhat at that range.

Centering the fine cross hairs of the sight on the rabbit, I did some quick mental calculating. The rifle was sighted in to impact on target at 250 yards, which meant it wouldn't drop more than an inch or two at 280 yards.

All this required precious few seconds. When you've done much varmint shooting you subconsciously chase much data through your mind and make whatever corrections necessary as

43

Binoculars aid in locating the quarry for long-range shooting. A flat-trajectory rifle fitted with a quality scope sight is a must.

you find your sight picture. I raised the scope slightly, centering the cross hairs right at the top of the rabbit's back, and squeezed the trigger. The rifle jolted against my shoulder, and the muzzle blast reverberated in the hot, dry Mexican air. The fast-moving bullet flattened the jack as a bowling ball would run down a pin.

Winston looked around at me and grinned. "Good shooting," he said. Immediately, he raised his binoculars and started scanning the prairie again, looking for another jack rabbit that might be out and feeding. I did the same with the scope sight.

At the time I thought how different this was from the jack-rabbit hunting I'd known in my youth in central Texas, where I was born and raised. I cut my shooting teeth on jacks, but it wasn't entirely for the sport involved. My dad was an avid fisherman. One of the very best baits for channel catfish, he found, was the liver and heart of a jack rabbit. So on our early morning travels to the Llano River we searched for jack rabbits, and it was my duty to collect a supply of livers and hearts with the little .22 rim-fire rifle we carried.

Now this was a special kind of rifle. It was chambered only for .22 Short ammunition, hardly the kind of weapon one would recommend for shooting tough and muscular jack rabbits. But since this was the only small-bore rifle we owned, it got the call. Dad wasn't about to waste one of his expensive deer-rifle cartridges on something like a jack rabbit.

For a youth in his fledgling years of hunting, it was most demanding shooting. Dad insisted that we get close to a rabbit, fifty yards or less, and that it was to be shot in the head. This prevented needless crippling of game, and anyway it conserved ammunition. Hit a jack in the head even with a .22 Short, and it isn't going anywhere but down.

Hunting with Winston and hunting with Dad, though done years apart, epitomized for me the appeal of jack-rabbit hunting. The sport itself can be as simple or as complicated as you wish it to be. You can stand off and blast a rabbit almost as far as you can see with a flat-trajectory center-fire rifle, or you can slip up close and plink one with an ordinary .22 rim-fire bullet, or indeed just about anything in between, from a handgun and a shotgun to bow and arrow. I've tried 'em all, and my hat goes off to the jack rabbit as one of the most exciting and fascinating of all off-season targets.

Jack rabbits are fairly widespread, being found throughout the Southwest, the western plains, and from Canada down into Mexico. Although jacks generally favor low, semi-arid prairies, some are found in mountainous country. A typical jack rabbit will range from four to seven pounds in weight, with some exceptional specimens going eight, maybe nine pounds. Its most notable characteristics are long ears and pogo-stick hind legs, which propel it with an extraordinarily swift momentum. Often it will bound for twelve to fifteen feet in a single leap as it gobbles up ground with its long stride. Among North American four-legged creatures it concedes only to the antelope in a foot race.

There are two subspecies of jack rabbits, the black-tailed jack and the white-tailed jack. The former is the most abundant, often found in astronomical numbers along the western plains and in parts of the Southwest. The white-tailed variety is the larger of the two, but its range generally is southern Arizona and the arid desert plains of northern Mexico. The white-tailed jack sometimes is called the "burro jack" or "donkey jack" because of its conspicuous ears, which stretch eight or nine inches.

Although it is wise to check your own state and local laws before going afield, jack rabbits are unprotected almost without exception and can be hunted throughout the year. These ravenous creatures multiply so fast that natural attrition can't keep them in check. Jacks are gregarious animals, sometimes roaming in herds of ten to fifteen, and they have been known to range for five to ten miles in search of food.

I recall a classic example in the desert of New Mexico. While I resided in Alamogordo, residents there were constructing a golf course. But as soon as new sprouts of grass began showing on the greens, jack rabbits promptly nibbled them off. To counteract this menace, large "drives" were organized to eradicate the jacks.

We hunters, armed mostly with shotguns and .22 rifles, strung in a line and moved across the desert, flushing jacks from hiding under stunted tufts of desert bushes. Every drive would result in hundreds of slain jack rabbits. But it seemed there was an endless supply. Steady hunting for more than a month only kept the jacks in some semblance of check. There was no eliminating them. For every one we killed, another soon showed in the area.

This ill-fated case of jack-rabbit destruction nonetheless points up one thing about jack hunting to keep in mind. The rabbits are attracted to a new supply of food, such as wheat, oat and alfalfa fields. In my central Texas bailiwick we often prowl around the lush green fields late of an afternoon to intercept any jack rabbits that come in to feed. During peak years of populations, jacks are known to destroy an entire orchard of young fruit trees and completely wipe away a crop of watermelons.

A sporting way to hunt under such circumstances is to station yourself on a vantage point overlooking a field, perhaps a knoll where your view commands a wide stretch of surrounding terrain. Scan the countryside with binoculars until you locate a jack, then test your long-range shooting skill with a flat-trajectory rifle like the .222 or .243. Sometimes the jacks will be way out yonder, at ranges in excess of 400 yards, and it requires a skilled shooting eye and a precision weapon to score consistently.

In this shooting a quality scope sight is a must. A four-power job is adequate, but something stronger than six-power is much better. Even a 10X scope isn't unreasonable. The magnification and light-gathering powers of a quality scope make bullet placement at long distances more of a sure thing. I prefer thin cross hairs for this long-range shooting, these being better than a dot or post reticle for minute bullet placement.

Any of the .22 varmint cartridges are suitable for this type shooting, the .220 Swift, .222 Remington, and others of similar class. Also very good are the 6mm. Remington and .243 Winchester. These cartridges all develop muzzle velocities in the 3000 to 4000 feet-per-second category, which means they'll zip out 300 yards or more with a very flat trajectory. With such hot loads, extremely long shots, 400 yards or more, not only are possible, they are plausible.

But you don't have to sit back and see how far you can plunk a jack with one of these souped-up center-fire cartridges to enjoy the sport. You can scale your ambitions down accordingly to what you expect from jack-rabbit shooting. Many hunters tune up for the fall big-game seasons by potting jacks with their deer rifles. Although the extreme range shots might not be possible with an ordinary deer-hunting combination, certainly anything up to 200 yards is reasonable. The hunter who can consistently execute a jack rabbit at 200 yards with his pet deer rifle won't have any trouble whatsoever with a big target like the whitetail or mule deer.

A recent innovation has been long-range varmint shooting with handguns. Thanks to modern-day developments, the handgunner can stand off and plink a jack almost as far as he can see. Hot-shooting pistol calibers like the .221 Remington, .22 Jet and .256 Winchester and sturdy handguns which will accept such cartridges and scopes made specially for pistol use puts this specialized handgunner in the medium-range rifle class.

But some of my fondest sport has come while hunting jacks with a conventional handgun with open iron sights. This is very demanding hunting. The shooter must possess the skill and know-how to stalk stealthily within short range of a jack if he is to score with any degree of consistency. Almost like bow hunting for jacks. In either case, the quarry must be close, the closer the better. For handgun hunting of this type, I prefer a long-barreled pistol chambered for the .22 Magnum rim-fire ammunition. With bow hunting, I like a conventional hunting bow in excess of forty pounds of pull and broadhead hunting arrows.

The jack is a lean and muscular critter, tough as the environment it inhabits. The conventional .22 Long Rifle cartridges are not adequate for killing it, although the .22 Long Rifle hollow point is sufficient for the rifle shooter who, at short ranges, can call his shots. But for handgunning where bullet patterns are apt to be more erratic and scattered, something more potent is definitely called for. The .22 Magnum shows at its best in this kind of hunting. I prefer the hollow-point bullet since what little you'll sacrifice in accuracy will more than be compensating with the added killing punch. For the bow-and-arrow enthusiast,

The .22 Magnum is an ideal gun for jacks at medium range.

a blunt arrow won't bring down a jack unless it is a head shot. The broadhead used in big-game hunting is more suitable.

There are two accepted methods of setting the jack up for these close-range shots called for in conventional handgun and bow-and-arrow hunting: stalking or by waiting in ambush. Personally, I favor the former since it is more demanding and exciting, but in some circumstances the latter can be much more productive. Around an alfalfa field, for instance, the hunter can crouch in hiding, perhaps wearing camouflage-colored clothing to escape detection, and wait for the jacks to start migrating in the late afternoon to feed. With stalking, the hunter can

49

During the heat of the day a jack rabbit likes to rest in the shade of a bush.

pinpoint a feeding jack early or late in the day and try to slip close for a shot. Or at midday he can catfoot slowly across a bush-studded flat and look for the resting rabbits. A jack rabbit scoops out a slight depression in the shade of a bush, which may be nothing more than a few sparse stalks of grass, where it rests during the heat of the day. The archer or handgunner should move slowly and quietly, taking one step and standing still two, looking for the statuelike rabbits. Because of natural camouflage, a jack rabbit can be very difficult to detect in the shade. Often only its telltale ears will betray its presence.

Another favorite sport of mine is to pussyfoot across a flat during the midday hours and roust jacks from their hiding places. The idea is not to look for a sitting jack but rather to flush it out in the open for a moving shot. This is popular sport for the shotgunner. The logical weapon is a full-choke 12 gauge loaded with No. 2 shot shells. But to give this game a more sporting touch, instead arm yourself with a .22 Magnum rifle. A jack, when first spooked, will normally lope out across the prairie at half speed. The rifleman can usually get in one decent shot at the slow-motion target before it cuts on the afterburners and really wheels away double time. If you get a jack good and stretched out, you probably won't cause any damage except to your pocketbook. It takes a good and perhaps lucky shot to down a jack running at full speed, but you can burn up a lot of ammo and have a ball trying it.

The possibilities in jack-rabbit shooting are almost endless. All it requires is the ingenuity and imagination of a hunter to give it a different perspective. It can be a complicated, expensive sport, such as with precision long-range rifle and components; or it can be simple, cheap sport like with the .22 rim-fire and open sights. But anyway you take it, jack-rabbit shooting is fascinating sport that knows no seasons, a sport for every hunter, no matter what his tastes may be.

52   Jimmy Robinson.

Chapter Four

HOW TO SHOOT DUCKS
by JIMMY ROBINSON

JIMMY ROBINSON has probably done more hunting and used up more ammunition than any other hunter you could name. He's been at it for more than fifty years and still going strong. He has done all kinds of hunting with some of the world's leading personalities, but shows a decided preference for shooting ducks and geese. As an associate editor of *Sports Afield* magazine he travels to all parts of the world on writing assignments. His recent book, *Hunting Adventures with Jimmy Robinson*, covers a lifetime of hunting. Jimmy picks the All-America skeet and trapshooting teams each year and has attended forty-two Grand American Trapshooting Championships.

W ITH something like 1,500,000 to 2,000,000 duck hunters in the U.S. bagging from 8,500,000 to 14,500,000 ducks a year, the man who gets his limit has got to: (1) Be an excellent wing shot, (2) Own a gun that fits him, (3) Have the right equipment, blind, and clothing, (4) Know when and how to call ducks, (5) Have the proper dog to retrieve his birds.

The average duck hunter is lucky if he takes seven birds in a season. But the average duck hunter is not the good duck hunter. The really good duck hunter will take his limit every time he goes out, weather and flights permitting.

The average duck hunter is the duffer who makes one trip a year, then puts his gun away and never sees it again until the next season. No wonder he misses ducks.

To be a good wing shot requires intensive practice—if not on game birds, then on the trap and skeet field. The born shooter is rare, but there are many excellent shots who have developed their talent. Trapshooting is more suitable practice for the upland gunner, but skeet offers shots at angles that duplicate shots at ducks over decoys and on the pass.

I would guarantee any novice duck hunter that he can improve his shooting 100 per cent if he'll burn up just five boxes of shells on a skeet range before he goes afield for ducks. For one thing, his timing will improve, and timing is everything in wing shooting.

I've been hunting on and around Lake Manitoba for fifty years, and I know what timing can do for the duck hunter. In that space I've learned that no one can tell another hunter how far to lead a duck. There are too many variables to take into consideration: the man's reflex responses, the angle and speed of the duck's flight and its distance from the shooter, the wind's effect on the shot string, the humidity of the day—and many other factors.

You would need an electronic computer to mix all these factors and come up with the right lead for any given duck and any given shooter. Fortunately, there is a shooting system that takes all these things into consideration and provides effective results. It is called the "swing and pull" method of shooting.

Here's how it works: The hunter sees the duck. Without taking his eyes off that target, he quickly but smoothly swings the gun to his shoulder. Keeping his eye on the duck, he is only slightly conscious of the barrel muzzle out there in front of him. But he brings this muzzle in a swinging arc to catch up with the flying duck. Naturally the muzzle line of sight is traveling faster than the duck to catch up with it. When the muzzle passes the duck the brain orders the trigger finger to pull the trigger and the shot is on its way. The shooter continues his swing on past the duck in a "golfer's follow-through."

This method automatically compensates for any angle or speed of flight of a duck at normal ranges of twenty-five to thirty-five yards. The two essentials of the method are smoothness of swing and perfect gun fit. Try it some time, and see if your shooting doesn't improve. Never jerk your shot off at a duck or stop the gun in swinging onto it and past it. And by all means follow through on that swing.

I mentioned gun fit. It doesn't matter whether you shoot a

side-by-side double, an over-and-under double, a pump, or an automatic. The gun must fit you or you won't kill birds with it.

What is gun fit? It's a gun with a stock of such a length and such drop at the heel that when you throw it up to your shoulder and snug your cheek up to the stock, your sighting eye will always and invariably be in line with the barrel and looking right down the length of it. Every time, repeatedly.

If you are short-armed, naturally you need a shorter stock, and if you are long-armed, you need a longer stock. But putting the butt of the stock in the crook of your elbow and seeing if your trigger finger can reach the trigger comfortably is *not* the way to determine proper stock length. No one ever shoots a gun in that position.

Of course, if you're going to wear a lot of heavy clothes in your duck hunting, you'll need a little wood off your stock. In any event, it's better to have a stock a little too short than one too long. The long stock will catch on your clothing as you try to raise it smoothly and quickly to your shoulder, which you must do. When the stock catches, you've destroyed the rhythm of your shooting—the timing, if you please.

A short-necked shooter will not need as much drop in his stock as the long, skinny-necked man. In fact, a so-called "straight stock" without any drop at the heel will be best for short necks. Why? Because when the cheek is snugged up to the stock the eye then will be right over the barrel. If there were too much drop in the stock, the short-necked shooter's eye would be behind the breech of the gun, and he'd have to raise his head and take his eye off the target to shoot. That's disastrous. Only many trials with many guns can tell you the stock length and drop for you.

While we're on the subject of guns, ducks have been killed with .410s, 28s, and 20-gauge shotguns. But my experience tells me the average duck hunter can't center the target well enough to make these bores effective. He is causing too many crippling losses. He needs all the shot he can get out at that bird, and for this reason, even after many years of duck hunting I stay with the 12 gauge.

A lot of experienced duck hunters swear by Magnum loads,

A good blind is a must in duck hunting. It should be built from the same native cover or materials in which you are hunting. (*Canadian Government Travel Bureau photo*)

but they're all Deadeye Dicks. They use the extra power to get more pellets out farther. The average duck hunter isn't a good enough wing shot to use Magnum loads. He'll do much better with ordinary high-base game loads at ranges he knows he can hit ducks in. Leave the forty- and forty-five-yard shots for the experts.

A word about shot size. In the early part of the season No. 6 game loads are fine. But as the season progresses and ducks get more heavily feathered and harder to kill, I always switch to No. 4 shot. It penetrates a little better than No. 6.

The two most important items of equipment are decoys and

your duckboat. The big thing to remember about decoys is that they should be an imitation of the species you're hunting. And they should be one and a half times the size of the duck they imitate so as to be seen easily from the air and from afar.

Of course, pintails, baldpates, and gadwalls will respond to mallard decoys, but mallards respond best. These are the "puddle" species, and often they will come in to as few as a dozen decoys. Generally speaking, however, the bigger the flights of ducks you're seeing, the bigger the decoy spread you'll need.

However, you can't just toss out a bunch of decoys and hope for the best. You can scare ducks away with a decoy spread too. First thing to consider is the wind. Ducks always alight into the wind, so place your decoys so that the open spot in your spread, where the birds will alight, is reachable with shot from your blind.

I've always been partial to the fishhook or "J" formation for decoys. For mallards and other puddle ducks I point the hook portion inward close to the blind, with the shank of the "J" running outward, because these ducks like to alight shoreward of other ducks.

The "J" hook is just reversed for the diving ducks because they like to alight in deeper water and outside of other ducks. Besides, the divers, like bluebills, goldeneyes, canvasbacks, and redheads, feed in deeper water, and this setup gives them the opportunity.

As I've said, an imitation of the species you're hunting is desirable, but not absolutely necessary. I've had bluebills come into oilcans painted dull black, and to headless blocks of balsa of the same color. Canvasbacks and redheads are quite a bit more particular about what they'll accept in decoys. It's best to have some of these species in your bluebill decoys.

For all diving ducks you'll need a much larger spread than for the puddle ducks. I've hunted broadbills on Chesapeake Bay where as many as two hundred decoys were set out. The divers generally fly in big flocks and they respond best to big spreads of decoys.

A few things to note about decoys: Never, but never, allow one to ride upside down in your spread. If it isn't riding right, fix it or remove it. And never permit a rolling decoy on the layout. Ducks don't roll from side to side with the waves. They bob up and down. So should your decoys. Finally, a little sunlight reflected off a shiny decoy will scare ducks faster than anything. If you have any shiny decoys, rub them down with sandpaper or finish them with flat varnish.

The word on duckboats is simple. Get one of the new aluminum duckboats with built-in flotation. It won't sink, and you can break ice an inch thick for a mile with it. Try to break ice with a wooden boat. You'll be taking in water in fifty yards. The ice simply chews away the bow stem and prow.

The one cardinal rule to remember on blinds is: Build yours out of the native cover in which you are hunting. Use rushes when hunting in rushes, rocks when hunting rocky points. If you're on a sand dune, dig a pit in the sand for your hide.

A blind should not be so high that you can't shoot over it when standing. But it should be tall enough to hide you completely when you squat down as ducks come in. Remember, too, that ducks can see down into your blind. So partially cover the top, leaving just enough opening to stand up with gun freedom to shoot.

Good duck calling is a great asset, especially to the mallard shooter. This species responds best of all to calls. The diving species respond little to calling, or not at all.

There are many good calls on the market, but they differ widely in tone. The best have a low, raspy sound that most closely resembles the mallard in its native habitat.

There are three basic calls for mallards, and they work occasionally on other puddle ducks. The first is the highball, used to get the attention of birds far away. It's a long, loud series of quacks which start high and run down the scale with increasing rapidity to a series of low, dragged-out notes.

When ducks respond and head your way, give them the "greeting" call. This is similar to the highball but speeded up and more excited. When ducks start setting their wings to come in, the "chuckle" is used. This is a feed call consisting of a series of triple-tongued clacks which tell incomers, "Here's a choice grubstake for you."

On a duck-hunting trip a good retrieving dog will save you work and money on shells and will bring back a lot of cripples that otherwise would have gotten away. (*Canadian Government Travel Bureau photo*)

The main thing in duck calling is not to overdo it. I've seen a lot of ducks driven away from a beautiful decoy setup in front of a perfect blind by some fool blowing his head off. If you don't know how a mallard sounds, listen to them on the marsh some time, or get one of the teaching records on the market, or learn firsthand from a veteran caller.

There's no need to tell the duck hunter to dress warmly. He knows that. But I do want to say that he could probably improve his score if he would buy one of those new camouflage suits now on the market; pants, jacket, and hat. They're so much better than plain, olive-drab clothing that there's no comparison.

For one thing, camouflage design on a jacket or parka breaks up the hunter's outline in the blind and makes him much more difficult to see. The camouflage hat is an added precaution, and I've seen some hunters go so far as to wear camouflage gauze over their faces so the ducks won't flare when they see those bright, eager features looking up at them.

Finally, the one thing needed to complete the perfect duck trip is a good retrieving dog. He'll not only save you work, but he'll save a lot of cripples for you. When you realize the average hunter needs five shots for every duck he takes home in the bag, a retrieving dog with a good nose is a conservation measure, and he'll save you money on shells. Besides that, you won't be repeatedly getting out of your blind to retrieve ducks and scaring the incomers away with your clumsy motions.

What kind of a retriever? Every hunter has his pet breed, but mostly it depends on the section of the country you come from. In the East the Chesapeake retriever is favored for his heavy, oily coat, his ruggedness in cold water, and his willingness to break ice to get at a downed duck. In the Midwest and on the Pacific coast they like Labrador retrievers, yellow or black. They're willing workers and they, too, can resist cold water. But it's doubtful whether they can take the really rugged going that a Chesapeake thrives on.

Irish and American water spaniels also make good duck dogs, but breeders of these species are few and far between. Golden retrievers are fine pets, gentle with kids, and only slightly less eager to please than Labradors. But their tenderness is against them in the rough weather that is the duck hunter's lot.

I've often been asked, "What's the toughest duck for you to shoot?" I always admit that the duck coming head on into your blind is the toughest. But early in life I discovered a solution for this shot, and I've used it successfully ever since.

When you've got a head-on incomer, wait until he's within

For a duck coming head on, wait until he's within gun range, then stand up
to make him flare up sideways.

gun range, then stand up in your blind. The duck will always
flare up and turn sideways to you, offering an excellent and easy
shot.

Another little touch I like about duck hunting; where it's permissible under the law, I always build my blind a day or two
before I intend to hunt in it. This gives the birds a chance to get
used to the new structure, and they're less inclined to flare away
from it when you move in.

So there you are, Mr. Duck Hunter. Now you know as much
as I about the sport of duck hunting in general. There may be
minor refinements in various areas. But in this chapter I've com-
pacted fifty years of duck-hunting experience. The rest is up
to you.

61

62   A. C. Becker, Jr.

Chapter Five

FOOLING SMART GEESE

by A. C. BECKER, JR.

A. C. BECKER, JR., was born and raised in Galveston, Texas, where, after graduating from the University of Texas, he joined the staff of the Galveston *News-Tribune*. He has been a sports and outdoor editor on that paper since 1946. He has hunted and fished in most of the southern states for over thirty years. But his favorite hunting is for ducks and geese, and during the waterfowl season he makes it his business to average three days a week of shooting. He has written outdoor articles for many national magazines and trade journals.

A SOUND like escaping steam, laced with frequent and high-pitched "gulps" . . . a shimmering wave much like the heat wave that rises off the desert at high noon . . . a wave that climbs and then moves across the sky like thin, wind-blown wisps of smoke—this is the description of a huge concentration of snow and blue geese vacating a field to head for new feeding grounds.

Snow and blue geese . . . waterfowl that move every fall into California, the southern states, and the eastern seaboard by the hundreds of thousands . . . are species that can cause a hunter to experience every emotion from utter joy to complete frustration.

Snows and blues were once regarded as "scrap" geese. That was back in market-hunting days, when the proud and majestic Canada goose spanned the nation in great numbers. Reduction of the Canada goose population to a piddling few has moved snows and blues up in the eyes of the nation's growing army of waterfowl hunters.

Snows and blues may not be as intelligent as Canadas, but

63

Geese coming in to rest on a Texas prairie. The geese in the photo include snows (white with black wing tips), blues (dark bodies with white neck and head), and Canadas (all dark, in the foreground).

they are still smart enough to make hunting them a keen sport if a gunner expects to score consistently.

At the beginning of a season they can be downright stupid. But once they have been shot-dusted a few times, they develop a cunning that can frustrate the average hunter.

In the first week of a season you can bag limits with the cheapest—and craziest—of decoys. I've pulled in snows with decoy rigs of newspapers, white rags, old baby diapers, and dozens of dinner-size paper plates sailed haphazardly in a field.

Consistent shot-dusting quickly changes that. By midseason respectable-looking silhouettes and full-bodied decoys are

Goose hunting requires big-bore guns. A full-choke 12 gauge with twos and fours for pass shooting and sixes for decoy gunning is the ideal weapon.

needed. And in the last portion of a season, particularly in areas with heavy gun pressure, even the best of store-bought decoys won't always fool them.

The very size of a snow or blue goose is what confuses the average hunter the most. An adult snow flying 100 yards away will appear to be about the size of a flying mallard 60 yards off. The average hunter knows how hard it is to drop mallards 60 yards off. So you can see what a job it is knocking down a goose a football field away. You might get one out of a box of shells with a lucky head shot or broken wing, but you can't call that sort of thing hunting.

So when should you shoot? Wait until you can see the bird's eyes and feet. Then, when he is bomber-size over you, cut loose.

This, of course, leads to the matter of guns to use and shot size. You're wasting time and money banging away with buckshot or BB loads, even though occasionally a pellet will score. Stick with 2s and 4s for pass shooting. If the birds are flying really low or working well to decoys, you can do better with 6s.

I've seen fellows hunt geese with everything from .410-caliber guns up to 10-gauge 3⅝-inch Magnums. Frankly, any gun smaller than 20-gauge is a poor choice for geese. These are big, hearty birds that require a lot of punch to kill. The small guns just don't have it, unless the birds venture by within twenty yards of you. And that rarely happens.

With 20- and 16-gauge guns the choke must be full. Modified choke is okay in the 12- and 10-gauge weapons because they throw a lot of pellets. But here again full choke would be better.

If you want to avoid goose water hauls, learn and practice patience. It can be more rewarding than a good hide. It means waiting for the birds to get within range. It means resisting the temptation to brush a mosquito off your ear. It means statuelike immobility.

You don't need a well-hidden blind, as you do for Canada-goose hunting. In fact, you don't even need a blind. With a big rig of decoys you can either sit down in the middle of the rig or nestle down in a clump of weeds or brush ahead of the rig. After that, just keep still. Most geese, when decoying, work near the head of the rig.

Man-made blinds are good for ducks where you need a good hide. Geese, however, will shy off from a good duck blind, since most of them stick too conspicuously out of the marsh or field. The important thing in snow- and blue-goose hunting is to stay close to the ground—and keep still.

Many hunters have taken to wearing white coveralls and caps, which are good when used in conjunction with a big decoy spread. Still there is a tendency for hunters wearing white to move about too much. I've always had better shooting dressed in clothing that blends with the field—while remaining perfectly still.

A half-dozen decoys will pull ducks within range, but a half-dozen snow-goose decoys won't get you a thing except wet feet, a runny nose, and a cold. The more decoys, the better. I've hunted rigs with as many as 500 pieces of newspaper or white rags, plus 200 store-bought foolies.

Snows and blues move in big concentrations. If the concentration outnumbers your decoys, you've had it. A rig of twenty-five or fifty decoys will pull in some singles and doubles, but all you can expect out of the big flight will be a few wind-blown droppings.

Decoy placement is extremely important. Naturally all the decoys must face directly into or at least quartering into the wind. On a dead-calm day you can face the decoys in several directions, although I learned years ago those calm days aren't worth the effort. But on a windy day face one decoy in the wrong direction and you'll open your gun just twice—in the morning to load it and in the afternoon to unload it.

Keep your decoys spaced eight to ten feet apart. Geese crowd up only when alarmed and ready to take flight. The best-looking decoys in the world won't pull in birds if they are spaced close together. Any geese such a rig pulls are (1) stupid juveniles, (2) gut-shot birds, (3) stragglers tired out from many hours on the wing. In any case, none are worth much as table fare.

Always place the best-looking decoys around the edge of the rig. These are the "watch" birds that interested geese look over the most. They rarely pay attention to decoys in the center of the rig.

Now is the time to bring up the matter of calls. Talk to ten goose hunters about calls and you'll get ten different answers. It's the same with duck callers. I've seen men win gold cups in calling contests and then fail miserably in the field. In short, the call that often sounds pleasing to the human ear can be a sour one to the bird on the wing.

This doesn't mean I don't believe in calls. A judiciously used call can be the difference between a water haul and a Sunday dinner. By judicious calling I mean the call should be used sparingly. Attract the birds and keep them interested, but don't overdo it.

With birds several hundred yards away, blow away to attract their attention. But when they're close, just give an occasional toot if you're located in the middle of the decoy rig. But if you're located outside the rig, shut up. One sour note from outside the rig pinpoints you for the geese—and they'll veer in the opposite direction.

Check a field carefully for decoy placement, and, if possible, do it the day before you hunt. Geese are birds of habit. Day after day they will work a field until it is stripped bare of edible matter. That is, of course, as long as the field is not hunted every day.

Take a 1000-acre rice field or prairie. The day before you hunt locate where the geese have been feeding. It's easy. You'll see lots of small white feathers on the ground. Don't spot your decoys where the feathers are. That ground has been picked over. So locate a fresh area for your spread.

Don't ever expect to bag geese by putting the decoys close to a stand of trees. Keep the rig at least 100 yards away.

In pass shooting, however, a stand of trees makes a good hide if the trees happen to be in the line of flight. Again use judgment. Geese won't climb for altitude if the stand is just a half-dozen or so small trees. But if it's a young forest, they'll climb to the clouds in passing over.

Now suppose there is a frequently used road—not a main highway—bordering the field. Many hunters would skip such a field, figuring the car traffic would spook the birds. Not the case at all. Unless it's in a section notorious for law-violating road shooting, that road and traffic can greatly aid the goose hunter.

Geese, though stupid at times, have great perception. They don't regard moving cars as any threat to security and hence will decoy amazingly close to a road. Some of my best shots over decoy rigs have been within several hundred yards of frequently used roads.

The manner in which geese work to decoys is very deceiving. Ducks telegraph their intentions from way out by the way they circle and cup their wings. If you know the characteristics of the various species of ducks, you can tell at a glance if the birds 200 yards out will work to your decoys or not.

But this isn't true with blue or snow geese. They may head straight toward the decoys or drift in from either side. They don't give hints of decoying or not until they're right over the decoys. Even then it takes practice to pick up these hints.

Let's assume you're hunting over a rig of 200 decoys. A gaggle a quarter mile away starts angling toward your rig. Suppose they approach at an altitude of 70 to 80 yards. That's long range, regardless of the claims made by some scattergun and shell makers. With some wild shooting you might down a bird. But that long-range shooting will wound other birds that will fly on another few miles before tumbling to earth to become wasted game.

If the hunting is early in the season, the gaggle quite likely will be a family group—two old or adult birds with their young. The adults are very white, while the juveniles are grayish in color. Keep your eyes on the adults. They are the leaders and they will make the first moves.

If the adults show signs of reaching for altitude, the gaggle is not going to decoy. One or both of the adults saw something wrong on the ground.

If the adults wheel sharply, they're going to decoy. The adults will be the first to land, and as soon as they hit the ground they'll start talking to the juveniles still in the air.

The birds might come down any place in the rig—in the middle, off to the sides, up front, or behind. This is most likely to happen on a day without much wind. On a really windy day, they usually decoy near the head of the rig.

When it comes time to shoot, pick the adults or leaders first. If you can get both, the juveniles often become so confused that they will mill over you, giving you additional shooting.

As a season progresses, families will group into concentrations that will often number a thousand or more birds. You're not going to pull in 1000 birds with 200 decoys. But there will be times when you have a half-dozen or so family groups in a single concentration work to your rig.

Again, watch for decoying hints. Snows and blues are talkative critters. At times a huge concentration will drown out all other sounds around. But when they're getting ready to decoy, the amount of chatter slacks off, and you'll note that all the chatter will be from the adults. Also, just before decoying the birds will bunch up, and the concentration will lose all semblance of formation.

Small gaggles wheel before decoying. Concentrations don't, although a few adults in the group might do so. Rather the whole group just starts coming straight down.

Snows and blues don't glide in on cupped wings like ducks. Instead they come almost straight down, tumbling and sometimes falling end over end. They'll catch themselves twenty or thirty feet off the ground to land right side up.

So much for decoy shooting. Now let's go to pass shooting, which can be extremely exciting. For this kind of shooting you need a heavy overcast with a lot of wind. This combination will keep the birds flying low.

In pass shooting you must be located in a spot that is between the birds' resting area and their feeding grounds. Determine this from the landowners familiar with the area, or visit the locale the day before you hunt and note the goose movements.

If you find an area with two big concentrations on the ground feeding, locate yourself between them. If they are a half mile to a mile apart, small groups of birds will trade from concentration to concentration throughout the day. Pick off the birds as they pass over you. Your shooting will not spook either concentration unless you approach too close or shoot directly toward either of the grounded concentrations.

Another exciting form of goose hunting is stalking. It's rarely practiced today, because most hunters know so little about it. And most of the fellows who do know the tricks are too soft-bellied and lazy to practice them. These days many people miss the real fun in hunting because they want to do everything the easy way.

Stalk hunting calls for a great amount of patience—and a complete disregard for getting wet and muddy. I've done three different kinds of stalk hunting with fine results. To work, of course, you have to have the right kind of weather conditions.

Start with the one-man stalk. This works well on a day with a lot of wind to cover sound, or a rainy or foggy day when

A one-man stalk is made by approaching into the wind and from behind the feeding geese.

visibility is poor. The approach must be made into the wind and from behind the feeding geese. The approach must be slow, down on your hands and knees. With patience and silence you can work to within thirty or forty yards of the geese. Then just stand up, shout, and pop off the birds as they jump into the air. There are two valid reasons for not shooting the geese on the ground: (1) It's not sporting, (2) Unless you get in a head or neck shot, a standing goose is hard to kill outright. Wings folded against the body will turn a lot of shot at forty yards. You might break a bird's wing, but you'll soon discover that a wounded goose can run much faster than you can over marshy ground.

Now take the two-man or hunter-car stalk. This is a whimsical way to hunt. It works in fields when feeding geese are a couple of hundred yards from a road.

71

The mechanics are simple. One man stalks the birds from behind. Again crawling is involved. The man in the car just honks the horn repeatedly. The birds will watch the car—maybe mesmerized by the horn—and become almost totally oblivious of the rest of the world around them.

Let me cite two wild, but true, accounts. On one such hunt I crawled right into a flock of snows. I got the wild idea of catching one alive. I inched up behind a big gander and lunged for him. What a brawl! He beat me with his wings and feet, knocking off my glasses, scratching my face, and tearing my hunting shirt. And on top of that he got away. On another occasion I moved to about twenty-five yards from a flock, stood up, and shouted. Two adults jumped into the air, and I cut down both. The juveniles became greatly confused and wouldn't jump into the air. They just stood there and looked at me. I had time to jack a fresh shell into the chamber and slip two more loads into the magazine. When they did decide to fly, I easily cut out three to fill out my day's limit of five.

The third stalk method can be used when your party includes four or more hunters. The hunter in front of the concentration walks back and forth making noise to hold the birds' attention. He never moves closer than 150 or 200 yards. The remaining hunters approach from the other three sides. The hunters on either side stop their approach about 100 yards out. Now it's essential that their approaches be made by crawling. The downwind man approaches as close as possible, and he is generally the first man to start shooting. When the birds take to the air, they'll fan out in several directions. Consequently the man up front and those on the sides will get in some pass shooting at respectable altitudes. Sometimes this additional shooting will cause a concentration to turn and mill about over the spot it just left. When this happens, fast reloading sometimes leads to a limit for every hunter in the party.

Geese have remarkable eyesight and when flying pick up suspicious movements from a long way out. A ranch hand walking across a field can be in the flight path of geese and have them go over him—within gun range—as long as he keeps moving and doesn't look skyward. But let him stop and look up, and the geese will immediately swing off to one side. Even if he keeps walking, they'll veer off if he points a hand, stick, or gun skyward. So the trick here is one of being nonchalant, walking with the gun against your leg until just a second before you swing to fire. This is no way to bag a limit of geese, but it can sometimes assure you of a bird or two on that long walk back to the car.

Regardless of whether you shoot over decoys, pass shoot, or stalk the birds, the weather has to be right. Right weather means foul weather—but not too foul. If the skies are bell-clear with not a whisper of wind, stay home—or go fishing.

Your best day will be a windy one with a low, thick overcast. This combination keeps the birds flying relatively low and is tops for pass shooting. A windy day minus any overcast or clouds is terrible for pass shooting, but it can be a fair one for decoy shooting early in the season before the birds become gun-shy.

Geese may be waterfowl, but a hunter would have to be a nut to go out in a driving rain. In heavy rain, geese bed down and ride it out. Your only hope of such a day would be stalking, and then you'd probably wind up with a case of double pneumonia.

A foggy day is good for stalking. It's also terrific for pass shooting if other hunters are in the general area to get the concentrations off the ground. Broken up concentrations will mill and trade back and forth looking for company on a foggy day. This is one day when you can blow heck out of a call, for even sour notes will cause birds to venture for a look-see.

For the most part on a foggy day, flying geese will be silent, moving like ghosts. They'll suddenly loom up in front of you and vanish just as quickly. It calls for quick shooting—and I might add quick identification. Many a fidgety hunter has clobbered a flying ghost, only to discover upon retrieving it to be a crow, hawk, or duck. Fog does funny things to the eyes.

Many, many people have asked me about snows and blues as table fare. The meat can be terrific—or terrible. It depends entirely upon hunting pressure and the time of the season when you get your birds.

Geese feed mainly on grain and to a lesser extent on berries. These birds are mighty fine eating. But in areas of heavy hunting pressure or late in the season, the birds will completely change feeding habits. They learn quickly where danger lies and will completely pass up choice grain fields where there is a lot of shooting. They will take to feeding on grass and grass roots. Then they'll take to feeding in the marshes. The flavor of the meat becomes strong when feeding habits change. Geese that feed in coastal marshes subject to salt-water flooding will develop a fishy taste.

Snows and blues range from four to eight pounds in weight. Occasionally a ten-pounder will be dropped.

Snow- and blue-goose hunting is a tremendous sport—and a sport that is likely to be in vogue for many decades. Poor nesting conditions in the northlands and expanding civilization have made serious inroads into the duck population. Snow- and blue-goose populations, however, have not suffered. If anything, the snow- and blue-goose populations have increased.

Apparently the only way their population can suffer will be at the hands of the hunters. But Garrulous Gus Snow Goose, a dolt the first week of shooting, learns quickly and during the course of a season makes dolts of many, many hunters.

Chapter Six

PHEASANT-HUNTING KNOW-HOW

by ALLEN GRAM

ALLEN GRAM lives right in the heart of pheasant country near Aberdeen, South Dakota, where he covered the outdoors and sports for a newspaper. Recently he accepted a public-relations job with the South Dakota Department of Game, Fish and Parks. He was born and raised in the same state where he lives and has hunted and fished since he was seven years old. Although he does all kinds of hunting, he gets a special thrill out of pheasant hunting, about which he writes so knowingly and clearly in this chapter.

AN OUTDOOR writer recently wrote that pheasants are the easiest of all game birds to shoot. He followed with an account of a South Dakota hunting trip where he and his companions wasted very little time in filling their limits. He left out one important factor—and that was, what part of the season was he hunting?

If he was hunting during the first few days of the South Dakota pheasant season, he probably had no trouble at all. But if he was in the field a few days after the season opened, his trip must have been a dream. Hunters who open the pheasant season in South Dakota have little trouble in scoring their limits. This early success is due to two factors: (1) Young roosters are curious and extremely careless; and (2) The older birds have forgotten the fireworks of the previous fall.

Indeed, it is safe to say that any sportsman who can reasonably handle and shoot his shotgun has little trouble bagging pheasants during those first days. It's after the birds become educated when the real sport of pheasant hunting begins.

A little about the gawdy and somewhat intelligent pheasant: first of all, he is a pretty tough customer. He can stand the

75

Allen Gram.

South Dakota winters with a grain of salt, even the temperatures that dip down to thirty degrees below. Like any other game, he soon recognizes the dangers a hunting season brings.

To escape, roosters will use hens for a decoy. I have had it happen to me many times. I see a crouched hen running into heavy brush. I dash in right behind her, hoping she will flush and bring up a rooster with her. She soon takes flight. I stomp further into the brush and wait. Nothing. Giving up, I head back. Suddenly I hear that familiar "cuckie—cuckie" sound that pheasants make. Turning, I see a rooster winging out of a spot only a few feet from where I had been walking. "Maybe some-day I'll learn," I think.

Noise plays an important part in the success of a pheasant hunt. Time and again I've seen it happen while road hunting. One of the fellows in the car spots a rooster, and everyone scrambles out—but the big mistake is made when someone slams the car door. It's enough of a warning to send the bird into the air before we have gone ten feet. Unnecessary noise should be avoided.

Pheasants can hug or cling to the ground like no other bird. They will use any available cover. Somehow they seem to pos-sess an instinct which tells them to stay on the ground because all the danger is in the air. So, in most cases they do stay on the ground until "kicked up."

Before we go into where to find them and how to hunt them, I would like to write a few words about guns. You join a group of hunters, and sooner or later one of them will be telling how his "old Betsy" is the best gun for hunting pheasants. Actually, there is no "best gun." I have hunted with several outstanding shooters, and they all used different gauges of shotguns from a 10 on up. A good friend of mine, Larry Debates, who is a water-fowl biologist with the Bureau of Sport Fisheries and Wildlife, almost always uses a 10 gauge while hunting ring-necks. One particular time, I remember, he had a string of thirteen birds going, including several doubles.

I personally use a 12-gauge Winchester Model 509. It isn't that I believe it is better than any other gun, but I prefer it be-cause of its light weight, due to the Fiberglas barrel. It is easy

The brilliantly colored rooster pheasant is on the left. The hen is drab by comparison. (*South Dakota Dept. of Game, Fish and Parks photo*)

to carry for prairie hunting or working draws in search of grouse. But it certainly doesn't shoot better than any other gun.

Some fellows, like Larry, prefer a 10 gauge while others like to shoot a 20 or 12 or a 16. The important thing is that you have the confidence in handling and shooting the weapon of your choice.

As in duck hunting, the most common mistake made by pheasant shooters is the failure to follow through on the "swing." If you learn to do this unconsciously, nine times out of ten you will hit your bird. Here is a suggestion for improving on doubles. When

The most common mistake made by pheasant shooters is the failure to follow through on the "swing." (*South Dakota Dept. of Game, Fish and Parks photo*)

more than one bird is flushed, sight in on the last bird to get up (if they're both in range, of course). By doing this, you will net more time. You can get one good shot off and then "barrel" your second bird without having to begin a new swing. In small flushes, I have found that roosters will fly together in the same direction. So conditioning yourself to shoot from "back to front" will bring you more shooting thrills.

What number shell to use? Most hunters are satisfied to use 6s. Once you choose your gun stick with it.

The main pheasant belt in South Dakota is located in the area bordered by Watertown on the east, Redfield to the south, Ipswich to the west, and the North Dakota border to the north. Aberdeen lies almost dead center in this area.

After deciding where to hunt, it is a good idea to get a map of the county or counties in which your hunting grounds are located. Familiarize yourself with the roads you will be using. Being able to move from one area to another without having to take time for stopping and asking directions can sometimes help bag a limit.

In South Dakota's main pheasant range, birds can be found anywhere from tree-shelter belts to ditches. But a well-planned pheasant hunt will include cornfields, stubble fields, and soil bank.

Let's take a look at each of the three fields. Cornfield shooting sometimes takes a little more organization to achieve success. But before you enter any area to hunt pheasants, remember to always work against the wind. The noise you make walking through the brush is less apt to disturb the birds than the wind carrying the sound you are creating. By working against the wind, you will be able to get much closer to the birds before they become excited.

No matter what size a cornfield is, it will almost always be sheltering at least one or two pheasants unless it was hunted only a few minutes before you begin. Cornfield shooting usually provides the most excitement because you usually can see the birds running in the rows ahead of you. You know that someone in the party should get some shooting. If you work the field at the right time, you can run into hundreds of birds.

The two important things to bear in mind when hunting in corn are: (1) The field should be adequately blocked, and (2) Never try to work all of the cornfield at one time if it is a larger one than your party can handle.

In connection with the first point, "blockers" are the hunters who cover or "post" the ends, and the "drivers" are the hunters who work the birds toward the end of the field. Both groups usually get plenty of shooting.

The better shooters in a group usually block the field. The number of blockers depends on the field's size. The two corners on the end, as well as the end itself, should all be well within shotgun range of someone in the blocking group. The blockers posted on the corners should be a good thirty or thirty-five yards from the corner proper.

The end shooters should be back quite a bit farther than this, at least from fifty to sixty yards. The reason for allowing such a gap here is because the end men will probably encounter the most difficult shots. The longer distance will give the blockers on the end more time to decide whether to hit the birds head on or let them fly past before shooting.

If the drivers flush a large number of pheasants, the birds will be zooming out at all angles and heights. It is difficult to concentrate on bringing down one bird when there are a dozen more in the same area. This is a very exciting moment, and a little cool thinking is in order. So the end blockers should have plenty of distance between them and the end of the field. Always a good safety precaution.

As the drivers near the end, the blockers should move around a little bit so the driving party will know where they are. This moving about doesn't improve the hunting, but it certainly may save someone's skin.

Members of the driving line should enter the field forming a V. The men on each end of the line should be several yards ahead of the men in the center of the driving line. This keeps the birds herded toward the center of the field. If there are enough hunters, the two end drivers should stay several yards out of the corn so that they have a clear vision in front and behind. In this way they can keep tabs on the corner blockers.

In working unpicked cornfields, the drivers should not be more than four or five rows apart, otherwise the birds will double back unnoticed between the drivers.

The most common disadvantage drivers face is caused by themselves—hurrying. They should not march straight down the field at a quick pace. Instead, the drivers should zigzag several rows, but this should be done in unison by all of them. If they see a bird or two running ahead of them, they should by all means keep moving and not stop. If a pheasant knows there is a slow movement behind him, he will try and stay ahead on the ground. But if the noise abruptly stops, chances are he will flush.

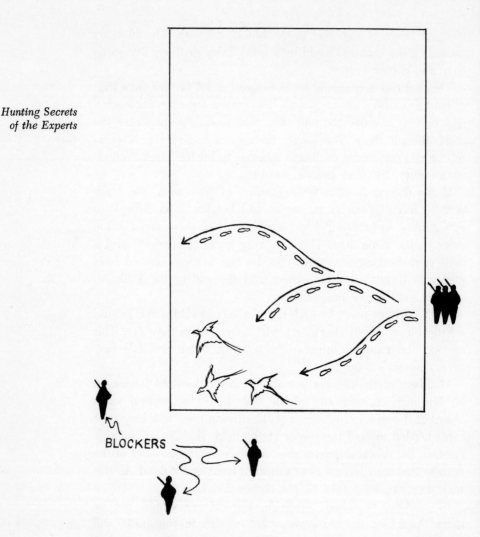

Six hunters working a large cornfield.

So drivers should try and herd the birds all the way, always glancing behind them. It seems that there are always some birds slipping through the line. Some of these birds will take to the air well within gun range of the drivers.

We always use a buddy system when hunting in a group. Before we start into the field, we all agree that the two shooters

82

walking next to each other will both immediately run to a fallen bird. Two pairs of eyes are better than one pair. And if you have a good hunting dog, better yet.

Many groups will ignore a large cornfield and look for something else. But they wouldn't have to. You can still do a lot of business by working just a quarter or a smaller section of the field. Pick out a corner and post one or two fellows on it. The others should then walk around the field until they reach the middle. Again working in a V, head for the blocked corner. Repeat the same operation on the other three corners and you will get plenty of shooting.

Stubble is the easiest type of field to work and the most ideal for using dogs. Stubble, which is the remains of picked grain, usually is about boot-high. While hunting in this type of field, you always have sight of your partners and you can keep a close eye on your dog.

It is always surprising to see several hundred pheasants flush out of stubble, because it is hard to believe that such short cover can hide that great a number of birds. Pheasants know their habitat very well, and they seem to realize that if they are caught in stubble there is no high cover in which to hide. So they will try every running trick in the book before they are forced to fly.

Work the stubble in large, wide, circular paths. Stop every few seconds and wait. If there is a bird near, sudden silence should flush it.

Setting up blockers in stubble usually pays off. Of course, as with cornfield hunting, don't try to take on too much field if there aren't enough hunters. Stubble is short enough so that a rooster can stick up his head and get a clear view of what is coming, which is something he can't do in a cornfield. And, like any other type of field, stubble should be worked against the wind.

Soil bank is the most difficult to hunt in both successfully and physically. It is a good idea to set up blockers, but this is more dangerous than blocking cornfields or stubble because some soil bank towers above the heads of the hunter, thus obstructing almost everyone's view except those doing the blocking.

When driving through "idle acres" be sure and have the end men on the outside of the brush. They should hunt several yards

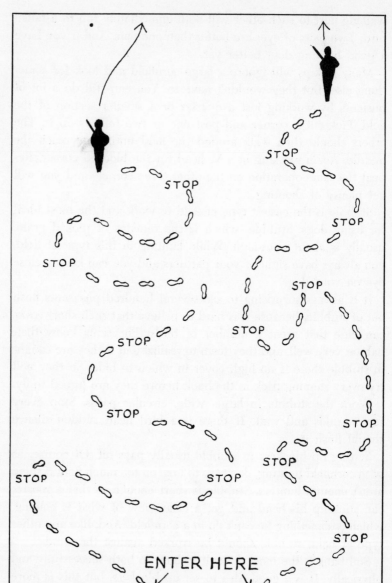

STOP

STOP

STOP

STOP

STOP

STOP

STOP

STOP

STOP

STOP

STOP

STOP

STOP

ENTER HERE

Two hunters working stubble or soil bank using "wandering" method.

out of the soil bank so they can get a good look at what is going on. A driver can be struggling in the middle of soil bank and never even know that he is raising birds left and right, because he can't see them through the thick growth. He is also making so much racket that he can't hear the clucking sound pheasants make when they take to the air. In short, a driver in soil bank can easily be out of it. The buddy system proves its true value when correctly employed while hunting in soil bank. Let me give you an example:

On one trip, in the late afternoon, five of us were hunting near Stratford, South Dakota. We were unable to get out until late in the afternoon, and time was running short.

We came across a picked cornfield which ran for a half mile. Walking it, we bagged only three birds. A gravel road ran adjacent to the end of the field. On the other side was a half section or so of rambling soil bank. We stood on the road, trying to decide what to do, when several pheasants flew out of the edge of the soil bank and lighted in the middle of the thick cover. Checking the time, we saw that we had only about an hour of hunting left. Ordinarily we would have never attempted to tackle such a large area of brush, but it was getting late so we decided we had nothing to lose. We checked our buddy system and then the five of us plunged in. The result was something I have never forgotten.

Keeping close together, we collected the remainder of our limits in a little over a half hour. There were thousands of birds in the field, and they were holding perfectly. What was really amazing was the fact that we were not using dogs, yet we never lost one bird simply because our buddy system was clicking perfectly!

So there you have the three types of cover, all of which offer excellent pheasant shooting. Needless to say, working a field immediately after another party has gone through is a waste of time.

All right, how can you tell if a field has recently been hunted? If you are in the field at the opening shooting hour, naturally you have nothing to worry about. But let us say it is midafternoon and you drive past a lush-looking quarter of stubble field. Have hunters been through it in the past hour or so? Take a look at

85

the shoulder of the road and in the ditch. Are there fresh tire tracks? This is where hunters will park a car. Then get out and look on the ground for empty shell cases. When you find some, take a sniff. If the case has been fired in the past hour, your nose will tell you so. But if the shell cast has been lying there longer you will smell only a slight powder odor.

Now we come to road hunting, which is nothing but driving a car down the road and looking for pheasants. Years ago this was the most popular method for pheasant hunting simply because that was all it took to get birds—a drive down a country road. In those days limits ran high and included hens.

When I was about seven years old, one of our neighbors used to road hunt every day after work and almost always took me along. We used to drive out around a cemetery near town. To a youngster in those days, the cemetery seemed about ten miles out of town. Actually it was only about three miles. Since then, the city has expanded to the cemetery's edge.

My hunter neighbor would simply drive up and down the cemetery road a few times and shoot his limit of birds from the car window. I did all the retrieving. This short hunt rarely took an hour or so, and I was always home in time for supper.

Once the season is in full swing, road hunting today rarely pays off. People still do it mostly because it is a chance for the family to get out together. Most road hunting is done on weekends. Getting a limit of birds road hunting takes most of the afternoon and a tank of gas.

One reason why this method is not as successful as it once was is because of the terrific hunting pressure that has built up since the late forties. Once the season opens and the lead has flown for the first few days the birds seem to seek protection more in the middle of the fields. And the soil bank or "idle acres" programs of the fifties has more than doubled the shelter that the birds need.

Here are some things to remember if you decide to try a little road hunting. Keep the car at a moderate speed so that you can clearly make out objects in the ditches or on the edges of the fields. If the ground is blurring, you are driving too fast.

Hunters in the front seat of the car should keep an eye on the road up ahead. A good 80 per cent of the pheasants bagged by road hunting are usually spotted walking across the road.

When you see a bird in the brush, drive several yards past the area where it was spotted. Then get out and run, don't walk to the spot. If the bird doesn't flush right away, keep working. It won't be far away. Usually a pheasant will fly when you first reach the ditch.

If you see a hen while you're driving along, stop the car, get out, and flush her. Almost every time she will have a rooster or two around her.

Always make sure a bird is dead before you put it in the car trunk or car carrier. Wring its neck for a good five seconds. On one hunting trip, we stopped the car, shot a bird, and tossed it in the trunk. We didn't drive very far when we got another one. We were all out of the car shooting the breeze while one of our party went to retrieve the fallen bird. He came back with it, joined in the conversation, and put his gun down. We finally decided to move on. He opened the car trunk to store the pheasant, and, whiz!—bird No. 1 flew out and zoomed straight down the road. None of us had our guns ready to use, so we all just stood there with our mouths open.

Being familiar with the country you are hunting is especially important if you road hunt. The county map will usually show you where the gravel roads and trails are which is what you want for road hunting.

And there you have the main methods of pheasant hunting. The novice will have to make a number of hunting trips before he will get the true "feel" and know-how of hunting ring-necks.

But he has one thing in common with the most experienced pheasant hunter. When reaching the end of a field, just before the main flush breaks, the veteran is just as excited, if not more so, than the newcomer.

88   Charley Dickey.

Chapter Seven

BOBWHITE QUAIL
by CHARLEY DICKEY

CHARLEY DICKEY is a field representative of the Sportsmen's Service Bureau, a division of the National Shooting Sports Foundation, Inc. He serves as a free consultant to shooting-preserve operators, and his work takes him to all parts of the country. He has hunted or fished in thirty-seven states (including Hawaii), as well as in Canada, Mexico, Japan, and other parts of Asia. But while he enjoys trying any new kind of hunting or fishing, his favorite is wing shooting—especially for bobwhite quail. He is an authority on shooting-preserve management and has written on this subject as well as on hunting and fishing for leading publications.

MOST hunters think of the bobwhite quail as strictly a southern bird. Actually the sporty bob comes close to being the All-American for wing shooting. It is found as far north as Cape Cod and southern Wisconsin and extends into New Mexico. It has been successfully transplanted to Idaho, Washington, and Oregon. But no matter where you find the bobwhite quail, it is always great for dog work, famous for its electrifying covey bursts, and is top table fare.

In Dixie the quail has attained its greatest fame. In fact, hunters speak of the bob in réverent tones with the same respect they might accord Robert E. Lee. It is not unusual to hear hunters say "Mr. Quail." Most often it is simply called "bird" or "bud." Although there are hundreds of species of birds in the South, when anyone says "bird," everyone naturally realizes he is speaking of quail. Yankees go quail hunting; Rebels go bird hunting. Both take their hats off to this glorious flyer which so delights the wing shooter.

In Dixie every social stratum enjoys bird hunting, from the

89

Late in the afternoon a pair of hunters move in past pointing dog to flush a covey.

farm boy with his single-barrel to the wealthy plantation owner who spends thousands of dollars developing wildlife habitat and dresses in the latest English tweeds for each hunt. Although everyone loves and respects the bobwhite quail, it can at times be a maddening and exasperating bird. As with any type of hunting, if you don't know your game and how to handle your shotgun you can get thoroughly skunked.

It is traditional and reasonable to hunt quail with pointing dogs. Few people ever attempt to hunt bobs by stomping around and hoping to stumble into a covey. The bobwhite quail is the best game bird in America for dog work because it holds so tightly for points. A well-trained pointer or setter will hold a covey for half an hour or longer. Many a hunter who has lost sight of his wide-ranging dog has found him an hour later locked up on a solid point with a covey only a few feet away.

Pointing dogs are not only necessary for locating quail; they *make* a hunt, for there is no prettier sight than a brace of dogs standing a covey or a single. To some hunters the dog work is more enjoyable than the actual shooting. There's many a hunter who keeps five or six bird dogs when he can barely afford food for his own table.

So if you wish to hunt bobwhite quail you automatically become a dog owner. Or you cultivate friends who have good pointing dogs. The man who owns a brace of stanch setters is one to be cultivated and praised and more to be treasured than gold or silver.

If you are new to quail shooting, you will want to use a 12-gauge shotgun. If you are a good wing shot, then a 20-gauge is adequate. Since the bobwhite quickly swings into cover, the ideal choke is improved cylinder—you have to shoot in a hurry and need a fast spreading pattern. In much of the South it is traditional to use a side-by-side double, the chokes being improved cylinder for the first shot and modified for the second shot. Many old-timers ream out all choke, or saw off two inches of the barrel for a cylinder or wide-open choke. Shot choices range from 7½s to 8s to 9s. The first of the season they may lean toward the smaller 9s; later in the season, or on windy days, they may prefer 7½s.

Assuming you have at least one dependable pointing dog and the proper shotgun and shells, the next step is to locate the coveys, which generally average about fifteen birds. Under the pressure of modern civilization and changing agriculture, bobwhite habits have changed considerably the past two or three decades. They seldom range far out into fields and may even be found at times in deep woods. In late autumn there is usually a "fall shuffle," that is, the coveys may do a little rambling until they find suitable feed, cover, and water for a winter home, which they break up in the spring for mating. In good habitat,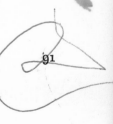

and if the gunning pressure is not too high, a covey rarely ranges more than a quarter to a half mile. Once you have located a given covey, you can return time and time again to the same area and find the birds. Naturally no sportsman shoots a covey completely out. When the covey drops to five or six birds it should be left alone for the remainder of the season to insure adequate breeding stock in the spring.

It is important for us to realize that all species of quail are short-lived birds with a high annual mortality of roughly 75 per cent, whether they are hunted or not. Quail *cannot* be stockpiled, and it is a waste of game if the hunters do not harvest a reasonable number of birds each season.

Coveys are generally found along edges—that is, where weeds or farm crops border escape cover such as thickets, swamps, or woods. The birds work out into fields for weed seeds, peas, milo, corn, millet, greens, or any of 600 different types of feed which they eat. They seldom move far out into a field and are generally within 150 feet or less of escape cover. Experienced dogs, as well as hunters, work only the edges and don't waste time in the centers of large fields.

One of the beauties of bobwhite-quail hunting is that there is none of this "dawn patrol" business. There is no reason to hit the fields at daylight. Experienced hunters wait until at least an hour after sunup to give the birds a chance to start moving toward the feeding areas and putting out scent for the bird dogs.

Under normal conditions the birds feed in the morning and again in the afternoon. The best time for finding the quail is roughly from 8–11 A.M. and 2–5 P.M. On an all-day hunt old-timers lay up from about 11 A.M. to 2 P.M., rest themselves and the dogs, and swap lies.

Where a covey is known to range but the birds are not found along the edges, experienced hunters will work up to 200 yards into the surrounding woods. They may find the covey loafing, sunning, or dusting in open woody cover. On rainy or windy days the bob seems to spend more time in cover.

All through this article the reader must bear in mind that I am writing about what happens *most* of the time. To take in all

Hunting Secrets of the Experts

The tail end of a covey of bobwhite flushing along edge of woods. The novice will do best if he picks one bird and stays with it.

the exceptions, one would have to write several books. For instance, a covey put under constant gunning pressure might quit the morning and afternoon feeding periods and make a hasty flight at noon to a nearby field of grain.

When the dogs *do* go on point in a field, then the fun really

93

starts! And so do the mental gymnastics. Most of the time you can figure the birds will fly toward the nearest escape cover. There are generally two hunters, seldom more than three, and they walk in line abreast *toward* the closest cover, past the pointing dogs, so that each gunner will have clear firing room.

The sudden explosive burst of a covey, as fifteen birds boom out together, unnerves the beginner. I have hunted bobs all my life, but the first few coveys each season terrify me, and I am not ashamed to confess it. I need a good deal of shooting every fall before my nerves settle down to where I can calmly enjoy the noisy covey flush.

The most difficult thing for a novice to learn on a covey rise is to make a decision which bird to shoot and stick with it! When fifteen or twenty bobs come exploding out of the cover at the same instant, the air seems filled with targets. You start to shoot one, but another swings across, and he looks easier; you balk, and before you can fire another looms up larger. As you balk, pause, grope, and become more indecisive, you finally panic and flock shoot, and the birds are gone.

I have been excited many times and flock shot at quail, dove, and ducks, but I've never yet knocked one down that way. To drop quail you must pick one bird and stay with it! When you make a decision, let it be final. The novice should not worry about doubles and triples. Concentrate on one bird and make sure you bag it. That will give you confidence, and later on you can graduate to doubles and maybe even a triple.

Actually the bobwhite quail is not a fast flyer. The noise and confusion of a covey rise, plus birds swinging in all directions toward cover, are part of the survival instinct which the bird exploits to the fullest. It's as much a part of his survival kit as his coloration, which blends so well with his habitat.

The mental capacity and reflexes of some experienced quail shooters rival any IBM machine. Here is what they will do in the space of three seconds on a typical covey flush. As they move past three dogs on point they will watch the style and behavior of each dog; they will pick up fifteen quail exploding into the air, will make a decision on one bird and drop it, then swing to another bird and knock it down, and next finish out a

When approaching a dog on point, hold your gun at a half-mounted position with muzzle pointing up.

triple; they will see which birds are shot clean and which may be runners, whether they are cocks or hens, how many times the other hunters fired and the number of birds they dropped; they will keep the dogs under control and at the same time watch where the remainder of the covey flees. And if you try to lie about how many birds you hit they'll catch you every time. I know of no other sport in the world where the mind has to follow so much in such a short time!

After the covey shooting, there is no hurry about following the scattered singles. It is usually best to wait a few minutes, to allow the birds time to put out scent.

In working singles or a covey, after you have shot once or emptied your gun, don't move until you have reloaded. Often on

95

a covey rise there will be a straggler or sleeper, and sometimes the singles land close together.

There is a proper way to approach a dog on point, whether he has a covey or a single. If you have more than one dog on point, it is easy to tell which dog "has" the birds and which are backing or honoring. With your eyes on the horizon and your gun at about a half-mounted position, with the muzzle slightly above the horizon, walk decisively past the lead dog or in the direction his nose is pointing. Your *ears* pick up the flush of the birds before you ever see them. This is the mental signal to bring the stock to your cheek; the muzzle is already on the horizon, or just above it, and barely moves. Your eyes are on the horizon, where the birds will be in an instant, and you are ready to choose a bird and fire.

If you walk past the dogs with your eyes looking at the ground, you will have to move your head when the birds flush and you are not as likely to get the gun cheeked properly. You will lose at least half a second, which is critical if you're in brush —or, for that matter, under most circumstances. Also, trying to see the birds on the ground—which is almost impossible—will slow you, since your eyes may "hypnotize" you as they try to pick up the bird when it clears the ground. The ascent of the bird from the ground to the horizon is so rapid that your eyes can hardly follow it, if at all. Look out ahead—that's where the bird will be in a shootable position and where it's easiest for your eyes to focus on it. Let your *ears* be the control center which tells you to click the safety off and mount the gun.

An obvious reason for approaching the dogs with the muzzle held up is that in case a gun accidentally goes off you will be shooting into the air and not at some valuable bird dogs.

When the dogs go on point, the novice tends to stand off to the side and wait for the birds to flush or the dogs to break and put the quail up. This is not good field etiquette; the dogs have been trained to hold and expect the hunter to do the flushing. In fact, if they're like most bird dogs they've probably had several tannings for flushing wild. If you are flanked way out from the pointing dogs, you are handicapping yourself, because you may be thirty or forty feet away when your partner walks in.

You and your companion should walk in briskly together, as though you're trying to step on the birds. The dogs, by their pointing and the direction of their heads, indicate where the birds are on the ground. Walk in for the flush right past the dogs. The closer you are to the bobs when they fly, the more time you have to concentrate on your shooting. In bobwhite-quail hunting you need every advantage you can get!

Bobwhite Quail

If you're new to bird hunting, the best thing you can do—as with any type of hunting—is to buddy up with an experienced hunter. He'll be proud to show you the tricks. He'll outshoot you for a while, but don't let that worry you. You're out hunting for fun and not for score. You'll both have your hands full outsmarting Mr. Bob.

And if you do take up bobwhite hunting the day will come when if anyone mentions "Bobwhite Quail," you'll take your hat off, place it reverently over your heart, and lift your eyes toward heaven in gratitude, suh.

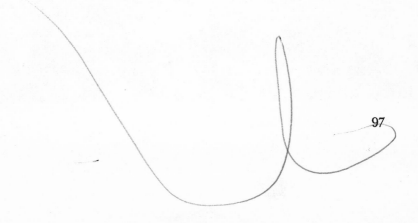

98   Henry F. Zeman.

Chapter Eight

RUFFED GROUSE

by HENRY ZEMAN

HENRY F. ZEMAN lives in Grand Rapids, Michigan, where he has been a staff photographer on the Grand Rapids *Press* for twelve years. In addition to regular photography work he also contributes words and pictures to the outdoor editors of that newspaper. Sometimes, when he goes hunting, he wears a camera on his back—a device he developed to record the many actions seen over a gun barrel. Zeman has been an outdoor enthusiast all his life and has sampled almost every type of fishing and hunting in his home state. His articles and excellent photos have appeared in the leading outdoor magazines.

TRADITION demands that the ruffed grouse be hunted with a large setter, stock steady on point, while the master moves up for the action armed with a classic side-by-side double. This scene is replete in woods dazzling with frost-painted leaves.

Tradition also decrees that the grouse, alias partridge, pat, thunderwings, or a dozen such descriptives be crowned king of the game birds. On this we give a hearty Hear! Hear!

But tradition be hanged. I'm an unconventional person and like nothing better than booting a few sacred cows along the way.

We grousers who are interested in Ole Ruff have digested page after page of information on this classic game bird under the guise of memorabilia and, like the gourmet, downed many an appetizer but never served the meat dish.

We lament the fact that through all this writing we find much misinformation, many old wives' tales, and just plain hokum. Much of the following is a localized look-see of the grouse in the author's pet covers.

Let's start from scratch; the ruffed grouse is a small handful, compared with the pheasant. Cleaned of its camouflaging feathers, it appears as if it were a flying wing. It is all breast mounted on matchstick legs.

The partridge is a creature of the woods—not deep woods, mind you—but, as it is best described, an edge bird. It spends the night roosting in trees, as do most birds. Then when the sun is up, it flies down to the ground for a day of wandering, feeding, resting, and dusting. Sometimes (rarely) when disturbed, it makes that jet-assisted take-off, so well known to sportsmen.

Time was, when the first white men appeared in this country, the grouse was as tame as the proverbial barnyard hen. But, to its unending credit, it adapted speedily, and today we have one of the hardiest and craftiest game birds. Even today, however, if you should go back to some parts of Canada, you may find birds that have yet to make this adaptation, and the natives drop them with a .22.

The no-experience beginner after grouse has an exhaustive job ahead of him finding birdy covers. How does he start? First off, the bird's requirements of food, water and cover. Key to finding birds is a supply of water close by. The best supply of food in the area can be nullified if no water is present.

This is how we first started hunting grouse. We pounded the banks of small streams till we blundered into a supply of birds. But soon we found this was not the complete answer. Not all wet ground is alike. When two links of the chain are missing, the birds are also. Some of the low ground may be cedar swamp. This can crowd out a lot of food growth needed.

The real kicker in my thinking along this lowland binge was the day I discovered a bonanza of grouse on the highest, driest section of land in the country. I had seen quite a few birds along this road during a summertime fishing trip. I marked this spot, and when fall came and my luck dipped, I hurried back and had fast shooting I have yet to duplicate. Two things attracted the birds. We had a cold spring, and the unending frosts killed all the wild berry crop except on the high ground. The water was here also; it seeped between the hills from a hidden spring.

Find the food and you automatically will find the birds close by. It's as simple as that. Whether they will admit it or not, most hunters follow this reasoning.

The ruffed grouse in its natural habitat gives no indication of the explosive power the bird possesses. In a split second he can be away in a woods-shattering flight.

What do grouse eat? Almost anything that grows in the woods. First love is some sort of a berry or seed. These are the food types the grouser should acquaint himself with during the fall season. Some of the berries or seeds that top the grouse's preference are the thorn apple (hawthorn), gray dogwood, acorns, blackberries (if the frost hasn't taken care of the crop), wild cranberries, wild grapes, apples—both wild and domestic. In fact, ruff eats so many different foods that in some years you might as well check the crop of the first bird killed as an indication of its food preference for the season.

I always follow this method. The first bird of the day has its crop inspected. Then I have a pretty good idea of what the birds are feeding on and where I can find more of the same. Sometimes, however, this can become a chore, like the season when all the berry or mast crops are laid low by early spring frosts. That's when the pat goes over to a diet of little leaves or other green tidbits it finds in the low ground. This makes for the most confused hunting.

Most of the time the bird will feed on one chief food that seems to be most prevalent at the time, or the ripest, or the easiest to gather. One day I may be looking for wild grapes, the next, gray dogwood, or thorn apples if there happens to be a good stand of fruit. Some eastern hunters claim this theory does not hold water. In their sections the bird has so many different kinds of food in the crop that it is useless to hunt food patches to find birds. But in the next breath they speak with reverence of the select apple orchard where they know a huddle of grouse are feeding. If this isn't following food patches such as I've described, I'll eat a grouse raw.

In the summertime the grouse adds such foods as grasshoppers, crickets, or other insects easy to catch. But it's rare in the fall to find such fare in its crop. That was why one year I was astounded to find birds crammed with oak grubs, a pest that had been defoliating the oak woods in certain sections. I went back to this location and had good hunting in the stripped oaks. All of the birds I killed had the grubs in their crops, in spite of the fact many acorns littered the area, and were untouched—they were on a meat diet.

It has been said the grouse is one bird that will never starve, even in the dead of winter. This I believe. The bird may be able to walk atop the deep snows with the snowshoes that grow like a burr alongside its toes, but it cannot dig down to food. That's when the big timber is its food locker. It simply sits hour on end in the trees and eats the tender buds nature provides. This is the mainstay of the grouse during the frigid season.

Some grouse hunters hunt with dogs and have good luck and endless sport. Others, myself included, hunt the critters without the services of the canines and prove to ourselves and others that it can be done. It is a fact, in spite of the tub thumping by dog lovers, that the bird can be and is hunted every season without dogs.

It's not that I don't like dogs; quite the contrary. It's that I accept fact as fact. I like nothing better than watching a *good* dog work its way through a wood lot and jam on the brakes in a body-quivering point while I walk up and flush the bird from the cover in a nerve-tingling brrr of its sonic flight.

But here are the facts as I see them. Pheasants can be hunted with all kinds of dogs, purebred or not. No matter what the breed is, it will help. I've hunted with a farmhouse collie that did a passable job. But take this line of reasoning into the grouse woods and we'll part company fast. The mutt or even a half-trained dog has no place in the woods. The dog must be good—period. Field-trial champ, pheasant snapper, or rabbit howler, it must be able to locate the bird by scent and point; and when the hunter arrives the bird must be here, not the location of where the bird spent the morning.

Another fact—anyone can flush a grouse. It doesn't matter what the intruder is—dog, deer, man, or cow. Get close enough and the bird will fly. The dog doesn't have some magical knack that keeps him bottled up till the gunner arrives. The dog with no grouse sense will flush a bird as readily as you or I. Add this to the knowledge that the hunter must be close enough to the bird to even see at certain times of the season, and it takes the bird a fraction of a second to vamoose. Then what good is the mutt that flushes the bird hundreds of yards from the gun? These are the facts I wish to infuse into the grouser's skin. I would recommend that the tyro hunt first without a dog. Let him learn where the birds locate and find the locations of the food patches, and I will guarantee he will learn more about the bird in three seasons than a man with a dog will in ten.

As to dog breed, it is difficult to pick the one best for grouse. The best can be a mixture of pointing types. I won't even go into breeds on this score. It's not unusual for the serious grouse hunter to go through a number of dogs before he finds one that suits him. It's not a crime to say your dog just does not have it—admit it—peddle it, and then go out and get another dog. According to those who know, the grouse is the hardest of all game birds for the dog to hunt properly. A tragic mistake many make is hunting their dog on pheasant one day and grouse the next. The birds are so different that it is cruel to expect the dog to perform well on both. A good grouse dog is hunted only on grouse. This brings out the best in him.

Even with a fine bird dog, the hunter has much to learn. You should be able to lead your dog only through those parts of the woods where food is available. The method of finding birds through their food preference also holds true.

The man with a dog has a decided advantage in strange territory. The hunter who wishes to explore new covers every day also has the upper hand. As a rule most hunters with dogs seem to stick to the more open woods. That is so they can see their dog better.

Without a dog the hunting is not impossible. I have my own pet method, developed throughout the years. In the woods, keep your weather eye peeled for food patches. Spot one; then slowly work toward the cover. When I get close, I stop, and with years of knowing, ease myself into a shooting position in case a bird is in the covert. I eye the cover; the sudden cessation of noise will unnerve the most cunning of birds, more than even the sight of the prowling biped. If no action occurs, I continue on. Each bit of cover is minutely inspected. Sometimes this may be a thicket of thumb-sized shoots, a windfall, or an overturned stump. Once I looked down into a burned-out stump and gazed into the eyes of a pat looking up at me. Yes, I missed . . .

Another day I rested for better than fifteen minutes at the side of a large brush pile. As I moved on, a partridge zoomed out. So that day I did a lot of resting at each brush pile I saw. It worked; it seemed each pile contained a dozing grouse. The grouse hunter should not drive game noisily through the brush. He should be more like the archer who stalks; he makes noise, true, but he is constantly on the alert. The grouser is inquisitive, he hunts likely-looking cover, looks for birds, and is constantly ready.

This has been said many times, and I might add, the grouse is the toughest shot a hunter can get. It is snap shooting at its best. And consider yourself lucky to ground one bird for each five shots taken. Most experienced hunters do better, or so they claim.

It takes less than a second, with foliage on trees, for thunder-wings to vacate your view. Often the bird clears the area without a shot fired. If you're lucky you may get two shots at the same bird. I've also seen the rare day when I had three shots at his nibs.

No one will argue the point that the partridge hunter needs all the help he can get to even the odds. I myself like the 12-gauge shotgun. My favorite today is an over-under. I recommend 8 or 9 chill in low brass; it doesn't take too much lead to tumble the grouse. One or two pellets of No. 9s can be his poison. When the leaves are down and the shooting is longer I slip in 7½s in the tighter barrel. Improved cylinder seems to be a good bore for this close shooting.

A few years back I downed a pat; before I picked it up it flushed again. I shot. Again it tumbled. I went over to pick it up and it took off again. I shot the third time and again it fell. This time I ran to the bird, caught it, and inspected the still kicking bird. The only sign of damage was one pellet, which had broken the key and feather of its wing. Later, while cleaning it, I verified my finding. One pellet that broke one feather was all it took to bring down this bird. While this was an unusual case, it does show how fragile the bird can be.

I proved this to myself years ago: the dogless hunter needs less territory to make a successful hunt. I believe I shoot at more birds that I myself flush. There are few wasted flushes. I

A grouse flies almost on his back as the powerful wings churn the air to get its body behind some cover and onto an avenue of escape.

took a friend out to some of my favorite coverts one season. I had a good idea how many birds each cover contained, also how long it took me to cover this territory. At first location, the dog was as wild as they come. All I could hear was grouse flushing wild throughout the woods. We followed, but not once did the dog strike a point. In ten minutes we were back at the car. I could have hunted this cover for better than an hour and had sporting shooting besides. This performance continued throughout the day, and it wasn't till almost dark before the dog made a classic point, giving the owner something to brag about.

I can take a 180-acre stretch of woods and, by carefully hunting, spend most of the morning there. Many experienced hunters return year after year to the same covers. They know where the food is, where the birds' dusting areas are, where they roost, and where they go to get water. They know the cover so intimately that at a given time of the day they can walk into the area and get shooting. This is the secret of many successful grousers. By multiplying these areas with four or five others, they can spend the entire season and never overshoot the areas.

Last year, I had a good chance to check this theory. The season opened, and because of my schedule at the newspaper where I work, it would be better than a week before I could go out. But by speedy driving, and gulping sandwiches along the way, I could get in three hours of hunting after work. I arrived at one of my pet covers in record time, changed my clothes, and went straight to a section where the dogwood berries were thick. I rarely failed to get birds up there. I had hardly taken two steps into the cover when the first bird busted clear of the dogwoods. I flipped up the gun, thumped off the safety, and watched the bird somersault to the ground. One flush, one shot, and one bird—I hadn't hunted more than five minutes. The end result of knowing cover and Mr. Grouse like the palm of your hand.

Now I'm going from stating that I know everything I need to know about grouse hunting to saying there isn't a day or a season the grouse doesn't show me a new trick. Indeed, when my golden anniversary of hunting partridge rolls around I hope I'm going to say in all seriousness that there still is a lot I feel I can learn about grouse. Pat hunting is like that. That's what makes it interesting.

Years ago, when I shot at grouse, I never followed through. I felt the bird I missed, or one that flushed wild, was a bird departed. Today when a bird is jumped I mark the spot where it

Rare is the time the gunner has the target in the open as here. Trees still may confuse the hunter as he lines up his sights on the speeding target.

headed, and when I'm through with the immediate area I go over to where it seemed to land. I discovered this tidbit: if I jump a pat in a line of poplars it will almost always head for the wedge of evergreens. And when I flush it from the evergreens it will head for the edge of scrub oaks. Explaining further, it always seems to have an escape cover all picked out in advance. Once you know, the action seems to be endless. But then this is the result of experience. Another bonus of the second flush is that it's apt to give you a better shot than the first. In fact, many a "bootstrap flush" occurs the second time around, so I've found.

It's amazing how many pat hunters don't know this fact—the partridge can't sustain a long flight. With the lightninglike take-off, the grouse soon burns himself out. The breast muscles of this bird just don't have the blood (it's white meat, remember) to keep flying. The flight of the bird is about a hundred yards. If you could jump him three times in rapid succession you could almost pick him up in your bare hands. I tried this little trick one year with the snow on the ground. I had one bird going toward the more open section of the woods. I never shot, just walked after it. About the third flight the bird was flying not more than twenty-five yards. I lost it when it entered a cedar swamp.

The partridge clear of the woods has been clocked at a slower pace than the pheasant. But it may take the pheasant longer to get going. What helps the grouse is the shock effect of its booming take-off and its ducking behind cover in less than a second. Quite often the tyro does a better job of bringing down the partridge than the experienced shooter; however, as he gains experience he falls into the same traps they do.

I can't remember the time I've picked up an article on ruffed grouse without some mention having been made of its "wild flight." Fall is the time of the year when this bird slams into all sorts of objects in a tipsy, drunken flight.

I can in all honesty claim that in all my years of hunting the bird, I have yet to witness this phenomenon. Frankly speaking, I seriously doubt if one in a hundred writers who write so extensively on this subject have either. All the birds I've jumped have flown straight and true—the only thing they have bumped into is my charge of shot—some, not all. I know that grouse do peculiar things, but taking off on suicidal flights is not one of them, at least not as commonly as is claimed. I think this entire subject is overdone.

Many fellow hunters I've talked with or read about pooh-pooh our dogless efforts at finding crippled grouse. The thought scares me not one bit. My lifetime score is very good. I've lost just one bird that dropped down into a woodchuck den. I'll even go so far as to call this aspect of grouse hunting elementary.

Why it is, I can but hazard a guess, but the thought of locating a downed bird even among dog owners sends the grouser into panic. One thing that scares them is that the feathers blend so well with the forest carpet. Honestly, the bird is *not* the runner the pheasant is—it's not like the crippled duck that scoots all over the swamp. Believe me, a downed pat stays put—if the wing is broken it's apt to make enough noise to lead a deaf man to the site. I only wish my score on crippled pheasants or ducks were half as good.

When I shoot at a pat and then definitely do not see it fly on, or see it drop, I walk over to where I think it should be. Sometimes I have been pleasantly surprised. But if I see the bird drop, I walk slowly to the spot, and most of the time I pick up the dead bird. Sometimes I do have to search for the grouse; then I mark the spot and look for feathers or other evidence of the bird.

The farthest I have found one from where it fell was not more than fifteen feet. I remember one day looking for one cripple for one half hour, then finally trailing it feather by feather till I found it ten feet away from where it hit ground.

There is one little trick I've seen the grouse pull so many times to date that I'm beginning to wonder if this little action confuses many hunters into thinking they have a cripple down when the bird is far away and kicking. The bird, on occasion, will fall at the sound of the gun, bounce off the ground, pick itself up, and tear behind the nearest cover and silently fly away. In the meantime the hunter nervously runs over to the site or shouts to his dog and spends the next hour searching for the cripple that isn't. I don't know if this little trick is planned or not. I think some birds will falter if a spent pellet hits or the charge comes close. This hesitation causes it to fall, and when it decides it is not hurt it hurries away.

I know some experienced grouse hunters will be quick to retort they have seen the bird fly on with a chunk of feathers missing. I admit I've seen this also more than once, but the above has happened, and it would be wise to expect the possum action at times.

Yes, these are the kinds of actions and tricks that send the grouse hunter muttering under his breath or reviewing the words learned in his wilder days. It's maddening, to be sure. The harder the bird is pushed, the smarter it seems to become. But then this is in its favor. Today the grouse experts claim his nibs can stand much more pressure than he is getting. Each year more and more hunters pick up their scatter-guns and discover the real king of game birds. In fact, the harder the ruffed grouse is hunted, the less tendency the bird has to die off in the ten-year cycle of feast and famine. Long live the king!

Ruffed Grouse

112   Bert Popowski.

Chapter Nine

THE ART OF CROW HUNTING
by BERT POPOWSKI

BERT POPOWSKI has done more to popularize the sport of crow hunting than any other man in the country. During the past fifty years he has shot crows in thirty-six states and Canada. His skillful calling and shooting have won him many awards at local and national crow shoots. He designed a crow call and brought out a Columbia recording of crow-calling instructions and demonstration calling. He has also written nine books and thousands of magazine articles on outdoor subjects. His books *Crow Shooting* and *The Varmint and Crow Hunter's Bible* are complete and authoritative.

EVEN if you don't care much for the crow, you have to give him his due. I've always had a deep, almost reverent awe for the raucous old rascal—the sort of feeling I usually reserve for space scientists and extremely angry women. For one thing, the crow has nearly every hand turned against him but gets along just fine. Men bomb him, poison him and gun him down, but he still flourishes and apparently there's not much we can do about it. There's a reason for this—the crow is just about the end point of avian evolution. He's gone about as far as a bird can go, and is splendidly equipped for survival under an immense range of diet and living conditions. Hardfeathered and sleek, he has a voice like a woodrasp and a mind like a diamond."

I've quoted the above from a chapter on crows my good friend John Madson included in his delightful book, *Stories from under the Sky*. To a remarkable degree John smote the literary nail on the head. Although I've aided in the demise of some 90,000 of the rascals I still encounter some situations where some crows somehow get the better of me. Perhaps one day John can be persuaded to join me for a top-drawer shoot, preferably during the spring and autumn migrating seasons, when we can further explore his comparison of crows to space flyboys and short-fused dames.

Basically, there are six main points of procedure which separate the regularly successful crow hunters from those who kill only a few, and then only occasionally. These should first be rated as equally important, though there are times when local conditions may make any one or two of them of paramount value.

Here they are: First, good calling to bring the birds within reasonable shotgun range; second, good "blinding" of hunters to achieve the same end result; third, building such blinds of verdure matching that of the hunting area and placing them in the flight lanes which quantities of crows will use; fourth, sensible behavior in such blinds to permit a maximum of called and decoyed crows to come in; fifth, using shot shells loaded with the finer sizes of shot; and sixth, being able to hit birds which can, when spurred by danger, perform an astonishing variety of aerial convolutions.

The first, fourth, fifth, and sixth of these points are inflexible if sustained success is to be achieved. Only the second and third are subject to wide variations, and then only when astute hunter-gunners are to perform in well-built and shrewdly placed blinds.

The hunter who properly appreciates the value of all six of these factors and trains himself to yield slightly on one of them for the sake of the greater returns another will give him on certain days, will bag a lot of crows. Conversely, the hunter who rigidly stresses only one or two of these factors as always being of paramount importance, and thereby discounts all others, will meet days when he simply can't buy a decent shot at crows within sure killing range.

In this article I am going to cover only the shotgun hunting of crows. There is such a sport as shooting crows with rifles. But there are only a handful of rifle hunters who kill as many as 300 crows per year, perhaps only a couple who down 500 annually, and I heard of only one who actually admitted to having slain as many as 600 crows during a period of twelve consecutive months.

In comparison—and I am here citing only my own personal experience and observation, not that of shoots which have been reported to me—shotgun hunting partners and I have twice exceeded 500 crows in single days of shooting, a dozen times shot 300, give or take 25, but literally have had scores of better than 100-crows-per-day shoots.

The best one-year toll we ever recorded was 4873; yet that included only two shoots of approximately 300 crows taken per day. Shoots of under 50 are all right for a shotgun hunter, but only if nothing more substantial can be found for any given day.

Such a comparison indicates that rifle shooting of crows is rather puny sport, if the quantity of birds taken is to be used as a measuring stick. Nonetheless, the precision requirements of rifles is so great, and so appealing to many sportsmen, that they would rather make one rifle kill than run a score of fifty crows with shotguns. Some of the most dedicated devotees of rifle marksmanship really consider "shotgun" a dirty word.

More detailed explanations of the six factors previously mentioned are definitely in order. Improved success is bound to accrue to any hunter who masters and regularly employs them all.

First, good calling. While it is true that infrequent flocks of untutored crows are encountered, the hunter who is after massive kills won't encounter such pushovers a half-dozen times during his gunning lifetime. Even then, with indifferent calling, he'll be lucky to kill fifty of such happenstance innocents.

Thus he must train himself in learning the calls which regularly bring in a goodly volume of targets. Next, he must be astute and skilled enough to adapt to local conditions where certain calls are most productive. And, finally, he must develop certain calls which, after a furious bit of shooting, will reattract the surviving birds.

All of the really good crow callers have certain things in common. They use pretty much the same rhythm in their calling. They point their calling at single birds, or flocks, with certain handling effects in mind. And they pitch the tones of their calls to suit their individual ability to continue calling as long as the birds are flying and supplies of ammunition and daylight enable

This is the end result of only two hours of shooting at roost-bound crows. A total of 124 of them were taken with only two shotguns operating over one caller.

them to continue shooting. No hunter dies a more agonizing death than the crow shooter who runs out of shot shells or daylight while a sizable supply of birds is still on the wing.

Calling must be of the "take command" type; not puny and anemic. Crows are loudmouthed and aggressive when they've really something to yell about. So the caller must imitate their belligerence to be effective, though shading the volume down, as his victims get close, by hand manipulation of the call. An occasional crow or two may get sucked in by a low, plaintive note on the call, but more out of curiosity than anything else.

In order to have crows come in headlong, they must be convinced that something is radically wrong with a fellow crow and that time is of the essence in giving it the asked-for succor. Crows that are completely sold on the authenticity and urgency of good calling will occasionally come slashing in within a very few feet of hidden, motionless gunners.

For 80 to 90 per cent of my calling I use variations of but two basic calls. The first is the furious, snarling "fighting" call with which crows announce the discovery of some enemy of crowdom—perhaps a great horned owl—and invite all fellow crows to come help tear this villain to shredded bits. Begun at full volume it is rather hair-raising in its impact, which is just the way it's supposed to be. It so raises crow hackles and blood pressure that the birds can't resist joining in and, what is most important, coming in to participate in the blood feud.

The second call is the come-back or highball call. It is chiefly used to bring back birds that have swung away from a glimpse of hunters or the sound of gunfire. It is amazing that so shrewd a bird will, if properly enticed, chiefly ignore gunfire in its overwhelming desire to have just one more look at what is causing all the ruckus. I have seen uninitiated crow hunters sit with mouths agape while the highball brought crows back into range even after they had been shot at and missed.

Using the come-back should not be delayed too long. For, if the birds have been fooled, turn away and get up a high head of steam, they are hard to turn back. Given too much time to think it over convinces them of what they think they've seen. But, if barely out of shotgun range, say 60 to 75 yards, or just out of sight behind screening verdure, they can often be convinced that they must have missed something. They'll then respond and return for another self-convincing pass or two.

The second important factor is the proper use of blinds. During the leafy months of the year, when natural cover is everywhere plentiful, blinds seldom need to be built. Crows are scattered then—in mated pairs, family flocks, and small concentrations—and massive shoots can't be expected. But that is an excellent time of year to learn effective calling, study crow behavior in coming to calls, and get some off-season gunning.

At such times one of the commonest mistakes of tyro hunters is to hide themselves so well that, although crows come in to

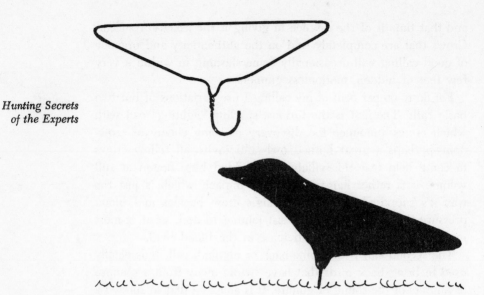

A wire clothes hanger, bent and covered with black cloth, makes a handy crow decoy.

their calling, they can't get in telling shots. Slipping under a dense, spreading tree is an example. Crows fly over that leafy umbrella and may even alight in it, but the gunner, unable to either see or shoot them has literally blinded himself out of participation.

Building functional blinds commences when deciduous trees begin to shed their leaves and continues on through the winter and the following spring. Whether it is of native growing vegetation or is man-fashioned, a proper blind should force the birds to expose themselves vulnerably as well as adequately camouflage the gunners.

A third factor, closely integrated with the preceding one, is the behavior of the shooters in said blinds. One of the very finest shoots I've called for—in which four of us, from high noon to full dark, tagged 556 crows by actual count—could have produced at least 100 more kills if we had left one jittery member of the party at home. The remaining three of us, seasoned in the niceties of the sport, could have shot all the crows this Nervous Nellie bagged and added a high proportion to those he spooked.

He was continually pushing at the blind, thus creating tattle-tale motion, taking premature shots instead of allowing the birds to come full in on us, and wildly firing at three or four successive birds when he would have run a better score of making sure of one or two. He wasted ammunition, spooked crows, chortled with glee at an occasional good kill, and generally was more hazard than help. Naturally, he was never again invited along.

This dude was the perfect example of how not to behave in a crow-shooting blind if a maximum kill is the object. Because of his silly antics a thoroughly heroic crow hunt was kept from becoming a masterpiece to remember for a lifetime.

Ideal blind behavior requires the hunter to stay absolutely motionless, his shotgun just inches away from shooting position, until the targets are nicely within range. Then one smooth motion mounts the gun, and its shot charge is almost instantly on its way. Jumping around in the blind for a better position, talking before or after the shot, belated reloading, or any other needless sound or motion is strictly taboo. The hunter who would kill a lot of crows, or even a goodly share of those called in, must abundantly realize that the birds have supersensitive ears as well as binocularlike eyes and use both with astonishing skin-saving efficiency.

So, in final analysis, no blind is any better than the sagacity of the hunters occupying it. The game-wise ones can make do with very little cover because they hold stump-still until game is in range; the nervous ones jitter away their chances at easy shots, generally can't make the tough ones, and have to "eat crow" when the moment for toting up their personal kills arrives.

Fourth, superlative crow eyesight must be foiled by exquisite judgment in building blinds that harmonize with their surroundings, don't bulk too large, and yet adequately conceal hunters, guns, and other gear. In a cornfield use corn stalks, brush and its foliage in a brush patch, and weeds in areas where they are native, easily procured, and look natural.

Using weathered burlap, sheets of camouflage cloth, or other artificials should be avoided since these fabrics show up as solid blocks of material color that appear unnatural in any but the rankest growths. They also tend to flap in any appreciable wind. In any density of cover sufficiently thick to conceal them it is a mere fifteen minutes of work to fashion a completely natural-appearing blind of the native verdure.

The hunter's clothing is also a part of his camouflage. Thus it's wise to pay close attention to the shirt or jacket and, especially, the hunting hat or cap. Crows detect colors exceedingly well, so a red or yellow hunting cap is something to be avoided. I've seen crows almost turn inside out in their escape flips when a red-capped hunter moved his head only an inch or so. Sticking sprigs of vegetation into a hat or cap-band is rank foolishness, since it merely increases the gross amount of visible motion.

A "bald" fresh-shaven face is another first-class crow warner, especially if it is of the office-bleached persuasion. Placing the face close to the material of which the blind is fashioned screens it somewhat until the hunter is ready to go for his shot. The best cure for "face-flash" is one of the fine-mesh face masks that Corcoran, Inc., of Stoughton, Massachusetts, sells for ninety cents. It both hides and shadows the face so the hunter's most visible feature needs only to be held still for fine camouflage.

Sometimes there's a quite different but equally valid reason for covering the face. I have hunted crows in such waterlogged areas as Canada's Duck Factory and elsewhere where insects were a fearful plague. At times it was nearly impossible to suck in a breath of air for the next blast on the crow call without inhaling several javelin-armed mosquitoes. They got into my mouth, nose, eyes, and ears and speared me everywhere that clothing drew tight enough so they could drive home their weapons.

At one National Crow Shoot I got talked into using a then popular insect repellent as a sure cure for the wee winged wolves. It was okay until I started to sweat. Then it ran into my eyes, nose, and mouth, where it tasted far worse than the mosquitoes. It also ran onto the palms of my hands and softened the varnish on my Ithaca shotgun to a sticky, gluelike mess. The gun had to be factory refinished.

Nowadays I use a preparation called OFF, which, true to its name, controls all bugs, from flying through crawling ones. The stuff may be sprayed right on the skin, though direct application in proximity of eyes, nose, and mouth is to be avoided. Spraying hunting clothing is generally sufficient to keep the hunter immunized for several hours.

Getting back to blinds and camouflage, it's worth noting that the shrewd crow hunter won't be married to some spot just because he has already built a blind there. As a result of changing weather conditions, of which wind is a highly important one, he may find it advisable to build new blinds for three consecutive days of shooting. Each time he will select a spot slightly upwind of the expected flyway which crows will use in the morning in leaving their nocturnal roosts for a day of foraging and for their reverse flight during the afternoon hours. Hunting a crowless area is like eating dry sand for the sake of the water it contains.

On several expeditions, after our blinds were built, strong winds sprang up, or prevailing winds shifted. Did we stay in those original hideouts and gnaw our fingernails? Hell, no! We moved, just as fast as we could, to more favorable locations, and thereby earned grand shoots.

One of the finest shoots was in an area where our original blind location yielded only nine crows in two hours; we shifted a half mile and kept our shotguns constantly hot for the next three hours. Another time, with gale-velocity winds building up, we left a beautifully fashioned blind and moved to a river channel which sheltered moving crows from the buffeting wind. They came in so low we actually killed a third of our birds by shooting down on them. I forget the exact kills at those two secondary sites but I do recall the first topped 200 and the second was well over 300. Which beats cursing the weatherman for his awry predictions.

Blinds should be suited in height to the height of cover in which they're located. Any blind that stands higher than a surrounding brush or weed patch is immediately suspect. To lower its height the shooters may have to go to their knees or sit on something similar to the wooden boxes in which we carry our ammunition. Standing upright in a tall blind is most flexible, for the shooter can then shift his feet and pivot for each shot, something that is harder to do from a sitting or kneeling stance.

Fifth, the use of small shot sizes. A crow is a relatively puny-bodied bird, though its color and its wide wings and tail give it an appearance of size far out of proportion to its actual weight. Size, of course, indicates its target area. So the hunter who used large shot sizes is bound to have a decreased number of pellets in given loads of equal weight. At any medium to long range the pellets will scatter so much that crow-sized holes will appear in the pattern. The net result is missed birds, or those that are hit with only a pellet or two.

Conversely, using fine shot sizes plugs up these holes in the pattern, automatically producing cleaner and surer kills, sometimes at astonishing ranges. The crow is really an easy-to-kill critter, providing it is hit. But many thousands of hunters annually handicap themselves in this fine sport by using coarse-shot loads—often with game loads more suitable for tough pheasants and big ducks—and lose a lot of targets that would have fallen stone-dead had they been smacked by suitable ammunition.

Let's look at it this way. The average crow weighs about a pound, about three times the weight of big quail, though a crow appears to be four or more times the size of quail in silhouette or flight outline. When hit, both birds drop without much of a struggle. No. 8 or 9 shot is generally used for quail. So, why shouldn't No. 9s—which, in skeet loads, are my favorite crow prescription—be an excellent choice for crows? There's really no valid argument against my pet shot size, or something very similar to it. But there are many objections to using coarser shot sizes, even in heavier shot charges of greater velocity, if clean kills at all reasonable ranges are the prime object.

I have never used No. 10 shot on crows, simply because it isn't commercially loaded. If it was, I'd use it. I prefer to spend my spare time shooting crows instead of hand loading the considerable ammunition such hunts require. But a friend to whom I expounded my theory of the progressive deadlines of fine-shot loads, hand loaded some No. 10 shot shells.

"You should try them!" he enthusiastically wrote me. "They really blow crows out of the sky at all normal ranges! And, on occasional long shots, they do as well, or better, than any other size of shot I've ever tried—including your pet 9s."

Item six, the final proof of skilled crow hunting, calls for adroit marksmanship. The crow is easily the most agile aerial acrobat in the avian kingdom. His broad wing sweeps and wide tail rudder can maneuver his one-pound body through an astonishing repertoire of twists, turns, dives, flares, and other flight convolutions almost impossible to describe. He can float on the merest breeze like a buzzard, ride a tail wind like a shot-stung teal, zoom like an elevator, or dive like a falling stone. (Among all bird flights he has only one failing; unlike the hummingbird he can't fly backward!)

The net result is that no one shotgunner can tell another how much and where to lead flying crows. That lead varies from one shoot to the next, even from bird to bird. The problem is further complicated by the fact that most crows are shot at against a backdrop of blank sky, where range and flight velocity can only be guessed at by the comparative size of successive birds. From then on it's a free-for-all, with one bird coming strongly on, another zooming, and a third going into a twisting fallaway. You learn to hit crows by shooting at them and missing often, until you master their full repertoire of shot-evading stunting.

Wind strongly complicates the problem, which increases with its velocity. A favorite crow trick is to sit up on its tail, to allow any wind full purchase against its broad surface of wings and tail. But what it does next is anyone's guess. The man with an excellent eye and a steel-trap memory for all these artful dodges will do better than one who shoots by basic reflex only. He will remember each maneuver and its solution, then apply it to the next crow that goes into that particular aerial routine.

I have gunned crows for over a half century. Yet, while duck hunting recently, with my Ithaca plugged to the waterfowling three-shot limit, I called in a lone crow to within a mere forty overhead yards. I cut at him once, but he flipped into a simple sideslip that carried his feet outside of my shot pattern, then resumed his cruise. I tried him again, and he sideslipped in the opposite direction. So I spent my third shot, at which he sharply eased up on the throttle and slammed on the brakes, so that my shot charge whizzed feet ahead in the direction his black beak indicated.

I suspect that damn crow had somewhere picked up some surplus radar gear, or that he owned superspeed telepathy. He foiled me so completely that I knelt in my blind and swore feelingly, yet admiringly, at that departing bird. I tried to tell myself that he'd slipped through holes in the shot patterns of those Number 6s. But with the Poly Choke on that Ithaca screwed down to full choke, that argument didn't wash. He'd just flimflammed me with three exquisitely timed and precisely executed dodges.

What is a good average on crows? The guy who collects one kill for every two shots over a period of several shoots is doing all right. The gunner who clobbers 75 per cent of the crows he shoots at—with one shot apiece, please—is in the expert class. On some days, when things go just right, he'll jump that performance by ten percentage points. But 85 per cent, day in and day out, is a perfectly tremendous percentage to run on crows. Which is a commentary in comparing trap or skeet marksmanship to crow shooting, where the 100 percenter hasn't yet been born.

One winter day, with ammunition in short supply, I bagged a crow with every one of the 177 shot shells I had with me. But that was a fluke. With plenty of birds on hand I ran that score by selecting the shots of which I was very confident on a strictly one-shot-to-one-crow basis. As sheer luck would have it, I guessed right 177 consecutive times. There were a few wobblers in that string, but before they passed out of eyesight, all of them collapsed. I've never done as well since, even to the point of bagging 50 consecutive crows without a miss, nor do I ever expect to.

Chapter Ten

WOODCOCK LORE

by HAROLD F. BLAISDELL

HAROLD BLAISDELL has lived in Pittsford, Vermont, for the past eighteen years where he combines a career of schoolteaching and outdoor writing. He is interested in all forms of hunting and fishing and finds a sufficient variety of these sports in his home state and nearby New England states to keep him active in the outdoors throughout the year. He has hunted woodcock for many years and is especially fond of this hunting because it gives a bird dog a fine chance to show his stuff. Blaisdell's outdoor articles have appeared in the top national magazines for many years. His book *Tricks That Take Fish* has proved very popular with fresh-water anglers.

W OODCOCK DO NOT resemble other upland game birds in appearance; their habits are distinctly different, and even their flavor on the table is unique. Although these deviations tend to set woodcock apart from grouse, pheasants, quail, and the like, they lend special flavor to the sport of woodcock hunting, and they also create the necessity for special hunting techniques. So true is this last that many a sportsman who lives in good woodcock country has never bagged a single timberdoodle, and there are even those who have never seen one!

This isn't quite as strange as it seems, for the woodcock is one bird which doesn't pop up just anywhere. In fact, very few are seen by those who make no special effort to find them.

This leads into one of the big secrets of successful woodcock hunting, one which breaks down into two parts: first, to locate those covers which hold the birds; second, to keep your mouth shut about all such finds. One is about as important as the other, and for reasons which I shall try to make clear.

Woodcock have exclusive preference for certain types of cover,

Harold F. Blaisdell.

and these are quite easily described. The woodcock's diet consists largely of earthworms, and his long bill and general anatomy are expressly designed for probing for these creatures. Consequently, woodcock usually congregate only where worms are abundant. Foremost of all such locations are alder thickets where the soil is rich, black, and moist. Such alder covers may be the alder runs which border valley streams, potholes, and ponds, or they may exist on high ground where slopes are kept moist by seepage from hillside springs. The next most likely covers consist of areas thickly grown to small birch, poplar, or a mixture of the two. Ancient orchards gone wild will sometimes hold woodcock along with the grouse such cover attracts, and swamps in which tamaracks are growing sometimes hold birds.

Spotting these types of cover is a relatively simple job, but there's a hitch to it. Out of dozens of apparently identical locations, woodcock will approve of and use perhaps two or three and scorn all the others. This means that you must poke about in a great many places to come up with a few really reliable and productive covers. Every dedicated woodcock hunter accepts this as part of the game, as indeed he must. He scouts his locality with two aims in mind: to learn where the woodcock are, and also to learn where they ain't.

Fortunately, this is a job that can be done piecemeal, and throughout the off season, for woodcock return to nest in their favorite covers in early spring, and they and their broods usually remain there until well into the hunting season. Should the native birds leave, they are likely to be replaced by flight birds about which more will be said shortly. At any rate, the cataloguing of productive covers in advance is almost a must for the beginning hunter, for otherwise he'll waste good hunting time slogging through covers which look promising but which haven't attracted a woodcock for years, if ever.

Scouting areas for woodcock covers is a pleasant enterprise which can be combined with fishing trips or with family drives along country roads. Likely-looking pockets will be numerous, but, as I have indicated, you are likely to strike pay dirt in only a small fraction of those you investigate. It doesn't take long to appraise a location, however, for woodcock leave easily recog-

Woodcock use their long bills to probe for earthworms. They leave tell-tale drill holes in the ground.

nized signs of their presence. Their droppings appear as white splashes, commonly called "chalk marks," and in probing for worms the birds leave easily spotted drill marks in the soft ground. These are obvious tipoffs that birds are present in a cover.

Prospecting is more fun when you take a bird dog along. He'll tell you quickly if there are birds around, and since you won't be hunting, you can turn full attention to correcting any serious faults he may be guilty of.

Some hunters go so far as to carry topographical maps and plot all discoveries thereon. I've never found it necessary, for any new woodcock cover I stumble on is one thing I'm not likely to forget—one of the *few* things, I should add.

At any rate, such newly discovered cover should be carefully noted, for it becomes a valuable addition to a precious inventory. And as any woodcock hunter will tell you, the less blabbing done about it the better. Woodcock hunters are usually kind and obliging souls, but this is one secret they withhold from even their best friends—*especially* from their best friends, in fact.

Such secrecy is well justified, for each cover usually goes on producing year after year, and private knowledge of the where-abouts of a string of such spots is a virtual guarantee of con-tinued good shooting. Each cover is likely to be small, some no more than pockets, and thus easily ruined by anything approaching serious hunting pressure. Regard for one's own welfare therefore dictates a policy of jealous secrecy, and it is the hope of every woodcock hunter that he will find neither strange footprints nor empty shells (other than his own) when he makes the rounds of covers which he regards as his personal possessions.

The regularity with which woodcock return year after year to the same covers is one of the mysteries of woodcock hunting. It is understandable in the case of covers of substantial area, but I know of several spots, each hardly larger than a living-room floor, which perpetually play host to a single bird. My partner and I visit these spots while making our rounds, and if we collect the lone bird another soon moves in to take his place.

Eventually we get the uncanny feeling of killing the same bird over and over, and we refer to each visit as "going in to shoot him again."

Woodcock are migratory birds, of course, and their migration is in progress during much of the hunting season. This lends additional interest to the sport, for, as I have indicated, a migrant flock may drop into a cover any night and thus rejuvenate the hunting. They use the same established covers as do the "native" birds that nest there, so the fellow who has taken the trouble to locate these favored locations will benefit from these flight birds as well as from the birds that spent the spring and summer there.

Woodcock may be hunted without a dog, but this version has never appealed to me. It takes dog work to make an interesting game of it, at least in my opinion, and my vote is for one of the various pointing breeds. I have a special weakness for dogs, which I have indulged by owning and hunting foxhounds, coonhounds, beagles, and bird dogs, and one of the chief reasons I hunt woodcock is the sweet thrill I get from seeing a dog strung out in a wire-tight point. And one of the reasons why I have special affection for the little timberdoodle is that he co-operates toward that end. Grouse and pheasants give any pointing dog a rough time of it, flushing wild, running, and pulling all sorts of ornery capers, but the obliging woodcock just squats and stays put until virtually kicked aloft. This gives a pointing dog of only ordinary talents the chance to zero in his nose, fetch up on point, and look like a champion.

For those who don't hold this particular thrill to be vital, a dog bred to flush game will put just as many woodcock in the bag provided he can be held in close enough to prevent out-of-range flushes. Cockers and springers are often used success-fully on woodcock, and retrievers—Labs, goldens, etc.—will do equally well, provided individuals are used that have an inborn desire to work up game as well as retrieve it.

Retrieving is an important part of any woodcock dog's duties, for it not only adds an extra element of interest to the sport, but it reduces the loss of killed and crippled birds almost to zero. My present setter is now nine years old, and to my knowledge she has failed to find only one knocked-down woodcock in the years she has hunted. And this was due to a freak circumstance.

She had pointed, and when I walked in a grouse got up. I had time for only one shot and missed. But the sound of the gun flushed a woodcock which took off in the opposite direction, and on this chance I scored a clean kill. Unfortunately, I didn't mark the bird down but merely ordered "Fetch!" My dog sprang to obey—but with the missed grouse in mind. Calling her back in did no good; each time I commanded her to fetch she'd go tearing off in the direction the missed grouse had taken. The whole affair quickly became a jumble of confusion, for it's very difficult to explain complicated situations to a dog, even one you've raised from a puppy. I never did find the woodcock, and my dog didn't do any better at locating a grouse which she believed to be down but wasn't.

But ordinarily downed woodcock are easy to locate, at least for a dog. Even wing-tipped birds seldom move far from where they fall, and their nearly perfect camouflage of mottled brown offers no problem to a dog's keen nose. Retrieving is another mat-ter, however, for some dogs flatly refuse to pick up a woodcock. Apparently woodcock smell good to a bird dog yet, for some unknown reason, taste horrid.

Such refusal by young dogs is not necessarily reason for de-spair. My setter would retrieve grouse while she was still a puppy, but it was several years before she would bring in wood-

A good dog makes woodcock hunting more enjoyable, but not all dogs will retrieve a downed bird, as this one is doing. Some dogs refuse to pick up a woodcock.

cock. She would find downed birds and stay with them, thus preventing losses, but nothing could persuade her to pick them up. Eventually she overcame this aversion, but she still retrieves woodcock gingerly, usually dropping each bird several times on the way in.

Woodcock covers are usually so thick that a dog is soon blotted from sight if he moves out any distance. It is wise to hang a small bell from his collar and follow his movements by the tinkle-tinkle. The sound of the bell will flush no birds, and it will tell you at all times where your dog is.

Since a good dog is so vital to the full enjoyment of woodcock hunting, some comment should be made about how to obtain one. Very few hunters are foolish enough to part with a finished dog, and trainers who offer them for sale are justified in asking a price which the hunter of average means can't afford to pay.

Probably the best solution is to buy a promising pup and work up from there. Since he should become a close-working dog, it is best to select a prospect whose lineage is of this type rather than that of the wide-going strains developed to meet field-trial demands. Breed is not important in itself, for a good woodcock dog may come from any of the bird-dog strains. To a certain extent, the Brittany Spaniel may be an exception, for this smallest of the pointing dogs has won special favor among woodcock (and grouse) hunters. This doesn't mean that there are no "goers" among this strain, but they have earned the reputation of being more generally inclined toward the close work that woodcock hunting requires. I have never owned one, but I wouldn't be surprised if my next bird dog turned out to be a Brittany. Several friends and acquaintances hunt them, and their unanimous enthusiasm has about won me over.

Developing a pup into a bird dog isn't the complicated process that is often claimed, for in spite of all you may have read and heard, inherited instincts play a much greater part than does formal training. If this were not so, it would not be necessary to start with a bird-dog pup in the first place. A collie would do as well if handling birds were something which could be induced by training alone.

If a pup has the right stuff in him, about all that's needed by way of formal training is that he be taught to obey a few basic commands. What's far more important is to feed him large doses of hunting, for once he's afield his heredity will take over—for good or for bad. If he's going to make the grade he'll do it instinctively, without undue fuss and bother. Of course, the somewhat unrealistic standards of field-trial competition demand a polish which can be accomplished only with intensive training, but these requirements have no great practical value for the average gunner, who asks little more of a dog than that he find, point, and retrieve. Any pup worth the feeding will do all three if you hunt him plenty, and what a blessing it would be if all chores were that pleasant.

A knowledge of covers and a good dog will assure you of shooting, but hitting woodcock is quite another matter. Here again they are unique, for they fly like no other upland bird. Woodcock get up close, usually right at your feet, and their air speed is relatively slow. They fly as erratically as bats, twisting and turning through cover that is always thick, and while some may offer easy chances, others will be extremely difficult to nail. There are men with superb reflexes who have little trouble with woodcock, but if your reflexes are no more trustworthy than mine you'll take your lumps along with your moments of triumph.

Notion has it that a stereotyped peculiarity of flight makes the woodcock an easy target—that he springs straight upward and then hovers for an instant before getting under way. The trick, so the story goes, is to wait for this pause and then take him. The big trouble, at least in my case, is that I'm always up against woodcock who seem not to have been briefed on this standard maneuver. Instead, they go corkscrewing off through the alders, buzz my head, and resort to other eccentric tactics which seem deliberately designed to catch me off balance. All too often, these are completely successful.

I doubt if wing shooting can be learned from advice and direction, even though these be supplied by a master of the art, which I am anything but. Natural aptitudes—speed of reflex, degree of co-ordination, and sharpness of eye—vary greatly among individuals, and it is only through experience that one learns to make the most of his allotted native abilities.

Although the actual act of shooting is a problem with no real academic solution, this is not true of the important matter of choosing the most suitable gun and ammunition. Advance selection of the correct degree of choke and proper loads gives any woodcock hunter an enormous advantage which he is quite free to enjoy.

Long shots are extremely rare because of the thick cover in which woodcock are found. Most birds are killed at ranges considerably less than thirty-five yards, and often when partially screened by brush. The best bet is therefore a pattern which opens quickly, and contains a maximum number of pellets to insure penetration of thick cover.

A degree of choke tighter than improved cylinder serves no purpose other than to handicap the shooter. Pumps and auto-loaders equipped with adjustable choke devices can be set accordingly with a twist of the wrist. I like a double, and the one I use was the conventional full-and-modified combination when I acquired it. I had a gunsmith open both barrels to improved cylinder, a relatively simple and inexpensive operation, and the resulting advantage has been worth many times the modest cost. There is a natural temptation to specify a bit tighter choke for the left barrel when planning such a move, but this is not a good idea. Second shots at woodcock are either taken at close range or not at all, and well within the limits of improved-cylinder patterns.

I'd vote for field loads containing No. 9 shot—but I use shells loaded with No. 8. This is because chances at grouse come often in the woodcock covers I hunt, and the No. 9 pellets are a trifle light for these larger birds. They are completely adequate for woodcock, and they would certainly be my choice in all covers where only woodcock could be expected. These tiny pellets will tumble woodcock as cleanly as heavier shot, and their great number per load results in a dense pattern which remains effective even when it is partially blocked by brush.

Scour the country, keep a dog, and fuss over guns and loads for a bird that weighs only a few ounces? Some solid citizens would look on the whole business as slightly ridiculous, and quite possibly they'd be right. Yet they could never sell this conviction to a woodcock hunter, much less break him of the habit.

He'll go right on ripping his britches in the alder jungles for as long as these covers continue to hold woodcock, for there's a special something about woodcock hunting that keeps a man coming back for more.

136   Roger Latham.

Chapter Eleven

HUNTING THE WILD TURKEY
by ROGER LATHAM

ROGER LATHAM started hunting at the age of nine with a single-barreled .410, changed to a 12 double, and now is back to the .410 for all his bird hunting except for geese, wild turkeys, and most ducks. Dr. Latham is a wildlife manager by profession and received his master of science and doctor of philosophy degrees from the Pennsylvania State University in this field. He worked as a wildlife biologist for almost twenty years and in recent years has been outdoor editor of the Pittsburgh *Press*. His knowledge of the wild turkey is based upon several years of research work with the bird, raising them on a game farm, and many years of hunting them in several states. His book *The Complete Book of the Wild Turkey* is considered a comprehensive work on the subject.

YOU don't have to be a genius to bag a turkey, but it helps. There's an old hill saying: "You have to be smarter than a turkey to kill one." After hunting these wily game birds a good many years, I'm just about convinced that old gobblers and old hens all have Einstein-type brains.

But seriously, to be a good turkey hunter, you need a gun capable of the job and you have to know how to shoot this gun; you should by all means have a good caller and know how to produce those whining, plaintive sounds of the wild turkey; you should know a lot about the intimate everyday life and habits of the turkey; and finally, you should learn how to dress properly, how to move through the woods quietly and slowly and how to sit patiently without moving.

A little luck on top of all these things helps too!

What kind of a gun? I use a 12 gauge with standard Magnum shells. The 3-inch Magnum isn't too much load for these big birds, but the gun itself is almost too much of a load for the turkey hunter if he's in rough country and walking quite a way.

The 16 or the 20 will kill turkeys, too, but the birds should be within forty yards or less of the gun before the trigger is pulled.

The size of shot for big birds like a turkey is always a debatable question. If the bird is called in close, say within twenty to thirty yards, you can hardly go wrong by plastering the head and neck full of 7½s.

But for ordinary ranges around thirty-five to forty-five yards with the turkey in flight, I'll take 6s or even 4s in the standard Magnum load. Anything as large as 2s should only be used in the 3-inch, 12-gauge shell, and I don't approve of BBs or any kind of buckshot. The hunter isn't being fair to the game in taking the long chance of bringing one down to stay with these oversize shot. Most often they merely cripple, and the bird gets away to die later.

What about a rifle for turkeys? Fine, I say, but it should be something quite a bit more potent than the rim-fire .22. These slugs bury themselves in a turkey's breast or poke a hole through the heavy white meat and do little more than make the turkey mad, at least for the moment. And he can be a mile away before he decides that it "smarts."

I'd recommend the .222 or something on this order. Even the .270 or other big-game cartridge is all right if it is hand loaded with a full-jacketed bullet. The common expanding bullet will make one big turkey-burger out of your trophy gobbler. The full-jacketed bullet is a good idea in any of the high-power .22s too. And then you shoot them either above or behind that big breast, preferably in the spine along the top of the back. Hold high, young man!

Which is the better choice for the average hunter—rifle or shotgun? I'd say the shotgun in areas where hunters are fairly well concentrated or when the hunter is using a turkey caller. When he has the country to himself and he's just sittin' and watchin', the rifle might be the better choice. I'd want a scope sight on my rifle and I'd want it to be a 4X, 6X, or variable power.

One thing sure, if you carry the shotgun, that big gobbler will stand like a rock out there about eighty yards and give you all day for a good rifle shot. But if you take the rifle, he'll flush out of a patch of laurel not twenty yards away and fly straight away as pretty as you please.

The answer to this dilemma, of course, is to get one of those nice over-and-under combinations with a shotgun barrel on top and a rifle barrel below. Trouble is, then you have to think up an entirely new excuse for coming home empty-handed.

Deer, elk, bears, and moose are color-blind, and you can go into the woods looking like an overfed cardinal, but don't try this with turkeys. They can see color and they can see hunters, believe me.

Remember the old turkey-hunter's adage? A deer thinks every hunter is a stump; the wild turkey thinks every stump is a hunter. Dress in dark-colored clothing, even camouflage clothing. I like the soft-cloth kinds so you don't make that swish-swish sound as you walk along. And when I'm moving through the woods, I spend more times stopped and looking and listening than I do in motion.

There are all kinds of turkey callers on the market. None of them are any better than the man using them. Some are no good, no matter who tries to use them. Even within the same make and style, some will be a lot better than others.

The man who purchases a turkey caller and doesn't take the time and pains to learn to use it properly had better leave it at home. If you don't sound like the real McCoy, you just naturally aren't going to fool that old bird you want. The best you can hope for is some late-hatched poult that doesn't weigh six pounds and hasn't learned the facts of life yet.

If I'm hunting strange territory, the first thing I do is buy a topographic map of the area. Then I study it and study it well. If you know anything about turkeys and a little about the forests you're hunting, you can get a lot of helpful information from the map.

In mountain country, as you might find it in Pennsylvania, West Virginia and Virginia, for example, you will see where certain small valleys will "head" in a bowl or basin near the top of the big ridge. These are prime spots for turkeys because they're often full of the kind of trees, shrubs, and vines which produce the best turkey feed. In addition, turkeys seem to like them for loafing during the day. I think, too, that they feel rather secure in these places well back from the roads.

I usually get up in the rim of the ridge, as soon as I can conveniently, and follow along it, calling down over the side into the top of these steep little valleys. When I call, I'm not bashful. I have confidence in my imitations and am not afraid that I'm going to make a false note. So I give them the brass-band treatment.

Many books and articles on the subject of turkey calling will recommend two or three cautious yelps and a pause of fifteen minutes before you try it again. I give a long series of yelps (nine to twelve) as loud as I can, and repeat this call a dozen times, perhaps, in the first five to ten minutes. Sometimes if the yelp doesn't produce a response, I begin to gobble on the caller loudly and insistently. Many flocks won't answer the yelp of the single bird (you), but the gobblers in the flock can't seem to resist answering the challenging call of another gobbler.

Many hunters believe you can't call a flock of turkeys and that you have to have the birds scattered first. Sure, it's a lot easier if you do, but flocks can be called just the same. The secret here is to make so much racket that the flock will be convinced that you're another flock. Of course, by racket I don't mean brush-cracking or banshee Indian yells but a variety of inviting turkey sounds. I often use two different types of callers, I make myself, at one time—the little rubber diaphragm caller in my mouth and the big box caller in my hands. I whine, purr, yelp, and gobble and am regularly rewarded by having flocks of three or four to a dozen or more walk right up to me.

Some hunters stop calling just the second they get an answer and never make another sound. This is all right, perhaps, for the man who is not sure of himself or his caller, because a squeak or other false note can sure change a turkey's direction in a big hurry. But I like to talk to them the whole way in and have called repeatedly with birds as close as ten feet without alarming them in the least.

I have the feeling that a good many birds who answer your first weak yelp lose interest long before they get to you, if they have to travel some distance. I can imagine their saying, "It must have been my imagination, I haven't heard another sound for over five minutes." Turkeys that have been scattered talk regularly when calling together, and it's normal for them to call every little bit. So I believe the hunter should do the same thing to give them direction and a little gentle urging to keep them coming.

When waiting for a bird to come, some hunters do everything wrong. By "everything" I mean that they can't sit still or lie still. They keep poking their faces around the stump or tree or up over the log to try to see the bird. But unfortunately for the hunter, turkeys can see a man's face move at unbelievable distances in open woodlands, and they will likely see you before you see them in thick stuff if you keep bobbing and weaving for them.

Stay down and keep your face behind some kind of covering such as leaves or grass, or even use a camouflage head net. I like to lie on my belly behind a log when the ground is dry and will stick a branch or two of pine or hemlock in the top of the log to hide the top part of my face. If I have to move my face or body, I do it as slowly as possible.

Never underestimate a wild turkey's ability to do a vanishing act at the last second either. There have been hundreds of birds that got away after they'd come within easy shotgun range of the hunter. Too many nimrods get "turkey fever" and can't wait until they walk close enough to be sure. If the bird hesitates, they begin shooting at fifty or sixty yards and often see their prize fly away.

I like to let the bird get within fifteen yards or fifteen feet. Sometimes they come closer than that, and I honestly believe you could grab a turkey's legs if you lay behind a log and let the bird jump up on the log in front of you. When you stand up at point-blank range, there's little excuse for missing, unless you really have a bad case of "turkey fever."

This brings up another point. Because I was brought up by a dad who was a real wing shot and who never let his boys shoot a bird on the ground, I can't bring myself to "ground scuttle" a turkey. I always stand up and shoot them going away, except in those rare cases when I'm carrying a rifle.

When calling wild turkeys it is very important to stay down and keep your face behind some kind of covering. If you must move, do so as slowly as possible.

It's interesting how different turkeys respond to a call. I've had young birds, who were apparently so "lost" that they were desperate to get back to the flock, run all the way in almost at top speed.

Others walk steadily in a beeline but without any unnecessary hurry. Some old gobblers will dawdle, stopping every few steps to look and listen, and you can be sure these fellows have been around awhile. With this kind you'd better not make any missteps.

I've had gobblers get so stirred up over my gobbling, though, that they would fly the whole way to me, often for quite some distance, and land almost on top of me with fire in their eyes. You almost have to shoot in self-protection at times like these!

The man who downs one of these beautiful big birds should certainly take care of it in the field so that it tastes right when it is turned up all brown and pretty on the platter at home. A turkey should be field dressed by having its intestines, gizzard, liver, and crop removed. The gizzard is one of the best parts of any fowl for me, however, so I empty it and save it. I usually put the gizzard, heart, and liver in a plastic bag when I clean my bird, which keeps them clean and keeps them from getting lost. The gall bladder should be cut out of the liver.

This field dressing is particularly necessary if the bird has been shot through any of its internal organs. Leaking intestines, stomach, or gall bladder will soon sour the meat through fermentation. If the bird has a crop full of berries, wild grapes, or other juicy fruit, this material will ferment and cause the flesh of the breast to sour also.

Some hunters don't know whether they have a gobbler or a hen, but it's no trouble to tell the sexes apart. Of course, an old gobbler should have a beard, long spurs, and pink legs. But a young gobbler won't, and it may be a "hen" to a lot of hunters. But just look at any of the contour feathers on the breast. If these are black-tipped, you have a gobbler; if the tips are chestnut or rust-colored, it's a hen.

It's possible to tell whether you're shooting at a gobbler or a hen, too, when they're walking toward you. The gobblers' breasts will look black, while the hens' breasts will be buff or light chocolate in color.

The age can be told by the feathers too. In the fall the young bird of the year, male or female, will have two or more of the central tail feathers longer than the remainder. In the old bird, all tail feathers will be the same length and form a perfect fan when spread.

The wild turkey is a real prize for the hunter because he represents the smartest, most elusive kind of game on the continent. The man who bags one of these grand game birds should count

Many hunters consider the wild turkey the smartest, most elusive game on the continent. They are extremely suspicious and have a keen eyesight.

himself among the truly blessed for two reasons—he has proved his prowess as a hunter, and he has been the fortunate beneficiary of a remarkable game-restoration program which snatched this bird from the very edge of extinction.

So, carry your bird with pride and try to make your trophy a gobbler if you can. Remember, it's those hens which lay the eggs to produce more turkeys for next year.

146   Bob Elliot.

Chapter Twelve

HOW TO GET A WHITE-TAILED DEER

by BOB ELLIOT

BOB ELLIOT was born in Massachusetts, grew up on a Maine farm and lived in New Hampshire for many years. He worked on newspapers, did free-lance writing and wrote news releases for the New Hampshire and Maine Fish and Game departments. At the present time he is travel director of the Maine Department of Economic Development. He lives in Augusta, Maine, and his work and hobbies of hunting and fishing take him to many parts of that state. His articles and photos have appeared in all the national outdoor magazines and many men's adventure and general magazines. He has also written two books on trout fishing and contributed to encyclopedias.

THERE is a simple formula that sums up "How to Get a White-tailed Deer": Go where they live, have patience, and make the first shot count.

If this seems too obvious, it is well to remember that only one out of every five hunters on the average drags venison back to camp during the annual open season in the forty-three states with whitetail populations—and, if further proof of this animal's smartness is needed, include the sizable herds in Quebec, New Brunswick, and Nova Scotia. Indeed, there is at least a scattering of whitetails in southern sections of most of the remaining Canadian provinces. Hunter success is shrinking fast!

Most recent figures give the United States alone a total whitetail population of nearly 14,000,000. Of the forty-three states, present density is called "excellent" in eighteen of them; "good" in twenty, and "fair" in only five states that have this species.

There are at least eight states that consistently maintain from 100,000 to 750,000 bucks and does, and many states with less area that have perhaps more deer to the square mile than even such big-name whitetail states as Maine, Michigan, Minnesota, New York, Pennsylvania, Texas, West Virginia, and Wisconsin.

Aside from the general methods of hunting wily whitetails (driving, stalking, sitting them out) there are less widely practiced techniques which have merit: the use of deer calls, the habit of backtracking, to see if one is stalking you! Or, as sometimes occurs, if deer are crossing behind you. It always is wise to look back occasionally, down that old logging road you are following; or to climb up on a rock or stump and scan the openings ahead on both sides and to the rear. Some hunters use blinds or stands in tall trees.

Before considering which method, or combination of ideas, is most effective, there are factors of perhaps even greater importance to hunter success.

These are (1) Food and (2) Cover.

In this regard, the hunting of white-tailed deer may begin weeks before a trip actually occurs! A wise man goes out pre-warned. He has written or phoned for up-to-the-minute information on just which common deer foods are most prevalent—and exactly where, in the current year. The source of such unclassified knowledge is one's state conservation department or forest-service agency. Often an agricultural department can also provide such facts. Indeed, a personal visit to field office or head-quarters (usually in the state capital) may establish a valuable relationship for the future as well. Game-management men in most states today are urging hunters to utilize the information they gather in their field trips. Certain areas may be overpopulated with whitetails and harvesting of deer there is encouraged by the biologists. It's like having a travel agency map out a trip for one's maximum enjoyment.

The same sources can advise a hunter on how to pinpoint cover that whitetails normally use. This is of far greater consequence in states that have marginal habitat for deer than in those with an abundant nature.

In northern New England, New Brunswick, Quebec, and Nova Scotia, for example, deer can feed on hardwood shoots, old wild raspberry bushes, acorns, beechnuts, and a variety of cultivated crops—to the dismay of agriculturalists many times. Apples, deer love; although most of the green beans will have died, open season on whitetails may coincide with certain grains and late clover patches still available to them. In the huge potato lands of the East deer also browse occasionally. They seek the cover of coniferous trees (spruce, pine, fir, and cedar) in this section for resting and sleeping.

A whitetail hunter should always remember that deer feed largely at night and sleep in the daytime. Thus, it is wise for the watcher and the sitter to be out early in the morning and to hunt until nearly dark in the evening. Those are the logical times for deer to move from feeding areas to their beds and vice versa. Northern deer browse heavily on cedar in the winter months.

In New York, Pennsylvania, and fringes of bordering states deer feed on white cedar, maple, ash, cherry, apples, sumac, and similar foods. They, too, seek cover under coniferous trees.

Southern whitetails lie down in the swamplands during the day and move into timberlands and cultivated fields to feed at night. Hence, the logical way to hunt them is with hounds, and this method is used in such states as Alabama with appreciable success and notable excitement.

Wherever he is found, the whitetail needs the protective cover of at least patches of forest land and, to browse in, cultivated fields, wild clearings, meadows, hardwoods, or certain shrubs and plants. Water is a further essential.

Specific information on the abundance or scarcity of common deer foods in any given season thus is of tremendous importance. "It's a good beechnut year"—"the apple trees are loaded" —"they've cut off the timber and the hardwoods are coming in at such-and-such a place"—a wise hunter absorbs such facts like a computer and calls them from his memory when he needs them.

There are a couple of other pertinent factors to remember about white-tailed deer. They move more on a rainy day or in the falling snow. In the late fall, when bucks are chasing does, they are further likely to travel by day. Finally, when jumped from their beds by other hunters, they naturally will keep mov-

A fat autumn whitetail buck that would excite any red-blooded deer hunter. The shoulder of this animal is not more than thirty inches from the ground. (*Maine Dept. of Economic Development photo*)

ing until they can escape to another haven—or return to their identical bed by a circuitous route!

With full knowledge of where and when to seek a whitetail, the lone hunter remembers that deer hesitate to walk downwind, so he enters the cover with the breeze on his face. He thinks that a deer actually is a small animal; that the vital chest cavity is hardly more than 2½ feet from the ground—unless the whitetail is bounding over blowdowns like an overgrown hare. If the deer is running, a hunter who follows him through the sights, leads on a broadside shot, and pulls down on the head and fore shoulder just as the feet meet the ground is the hunter who legitimately can brag later.

Stalking deer alone is one of the earlier methods of hunting. It seems likely that Indians were especially skillful at this. They followed game trails in their noiseless moccasins or traveled by canoe, watching stream and lake banks. Having learned that whitetails bed down on the warm, sunny side of a ridge or, in bad weather, in an evergreen thicket, the red man sought out such locations.

Deer were far less numerous before the heavy forests were timbered off. Early writers have indicated that when entire Indian tribes needed food they conducted large-scale drives. Fires were even set to force deer into traps, over cliffs or into the water.

When deer hunting became a sport instead of a necessity the conservation pendulum swung back and forth. In some cases deer have multiplied beyond the available food and have starved. For the most part, nowadays, populations are leveling off and hunting pressure is sufficient to keep herds healthy.

One highly successful method of hunting whitetails is that practiced in most areas of the northeast, particularly when a congenial group is staying at the same sporting camp. The technique is a combination of driving and sitting. A few highly knowledgeable guides or local sportsmen move through the woods, and the rest of the party remains on "stands" (in this case, a location beside an old logging road, or in a clearing, or on a high knoll where vision is good for some distance). The waiting hunter may be seated on a log, or he may have his back against a convenient tree. Whatever his position, he moves hardly at all. The moment he does, away goes a deer! It's not always possible to remain immobile. The air is sharp; sometimes freezing cold—yet he appreciates the importance of sitting still. If he sees a deer and his rifle lies across his lap in the wrong direction, he must make his movements with agonizingly slow care.

Experience has led some hunters to believe that the flashing shine of fluorescent safety clothing will startle a deer but that a scarlet wool coat will not, unless there is a decided movement on the part of the wearer. Many hunters prefer to wear clothing that blends in with the woods coloring—green, not gray or brown. The latter two are dangerously like the color of a deer. A decided value of fluorescence is that it can be seen for such great distances, and if a man is lost in the woods he can be spotted from the air for miles according to flying game wardens.

Frequently the slow-driving method is done in this way: the guides walk parallel to an unused logging road, and a considerable number of hunters are placed at intervals beside the road. (They occupy stands on the edge of the road, not in the middle of it.) Deer cross such openings of their own volition, even without being pressured. Thus slow walking gets them moving and they are not unduly startled, as they are in the big, organized drives practiced in such states as New Jersey. Again the type of terrain decides what hunting procedure is best.

An individual who possesses real patience makes a good lone hunter. Many such men have returned season after season to the identical spot where they killed their first deer, and by waiting them out they usually have scored again and again. One such hunter of the author's acquaintance followed deer trails up and down hardwood ridges in a rolling, mountainous section of upper New Hampshire on his initial attempt to down a young buck or fat doe (either sex is allowable in the Granite State). He jumped many deer but saw only their vanishing white flags. Tired and nonplused, he sat down on what the guides there whimsically describe as "a fanny-high falldown" (an old tree, uprooted by wind and lying conveniently on its branches, just the right height for sitting and meditating). He was almost

Dragging a deer is safer than carrying it on your back. There's less chance of being mistaken for a deer.

completely hidden from the view of other hunters—and from any meandering whitetails.

Perhaps an hour passed; he didn't remember exactly, in telling of his experience afterward. Anyhow, he heard a soft scattering of leaves, thought it was a squirrel, maybe, looked to make certain, and stared directly into the eyes of an equally startled

153

eight-pointer. My friend was faster than the deer, and one shot spelled venison on the platter.

Several weeks previous to the next open season, he went back to the spot with pick and shovel and dug out a small cave under the roots of the blowdown. While he could only watch the deer trail in a single direction from the shelter, that proved to be enough and he has taken a buck or doe out of the same location nearly every fall since.

His single-vision hideout is reminiscent of the philosophy practiced by many old-time duck and goose hunters. "Just sit still and watch the tollers (decoys)." They cared little for the whistle of wings, shadows overhead. Birds *in range* were their prime concern.

A similar line of thought doubtless causes many deer hunters to choose shotguns rather than rifles when in pursuit of whitetails. They know that shooting is apt to be close, often in comparatively thick cover. Buckshot doesn't deflect like rifle slugs; few chances at this species are beyond 50 yards, and for the 100-yard tries they always can fire the amazingly accurate rifled slugs from their favorite double, pump, or autoloading shotgun. Unless rifles are accurately sighted each fall by experts, and unless more practicing is done than the average sportsman finds time to do, then—even where rifles are legally allowed in whitetail states—the shotgun is a more dependable weapon. This is especially true on running targets, although there are thousands of men who prefer one of the popular deer rifles, of course.

When rifles are used, many whitetail hunters select a folding peep sight and a good, visible front bead in preference to a scope. There are many topnotch deer hunters who claim they need only throw the rifle to their shoulders and line up the deer through what seems to be a very large O (the peep) and that they do not *consciously* think about the front bead at all. Again it is largely a matter of preference. Nobody can detract from the value and added accuracy of a hunting scope, properly installed, sighted in, and used by experienced shooters.

For shooting at whitetails in such unique places as the big bogs in Washington County, Maine—where a hunter often can see for great distances—the scope is a valuable item. It is excellent to scan the surrounding area, too, although a pair of binoculars also does this job just as well. The scope or field glasses, can be helpful in finding one's way in and out of unfamiliar woodlands; either can be utilized to make certain that the target is actually a deer, not a man! With this in mind, one should always have glasses with him to make certain of distant or indistinct objects before pulling the trigger.

The scope-equipped rifle is valuable when a tree stand is used. A farmer friend in good whitetail country has fenced in about 1000 acres of his dairy land. The section has wild apple trees, hardwoods, berries. He plants grains there for his herd of cattle. Deer are abundant. In the open season, he allows sportsmen to hunt the area for a fee. They board at his farmhouse. Daytimes he has them on stands—*in* stands, sometimes—for he has sunken barrels in strategic locations, and the standing hunter's face is hidden by small boughs, as in a waterfowl blind. The farmer moves deer slowly along toward the waiting men. If they fail to score, he places them in a tree blind late in the afternoons and advises them to wait until dusk before they climb down. Here scope sights are a definite must. In states where such tree stands or blinds are legally allowed, many hunters build their own.

The relative value of using deer scent, calls, and other mechanical devices is a subject of debate in many deer camps. A sportsman should check restrictive laws to see if they are allowable in the area he plans to hunt, of course. When bucks are rutting, the occasional rattling of a pair of old antlers may prove effective. Too-frequent use of noise of any kind will drive most whitetails into the next county, but deer are curious, and in the late fall bucks are aggressive. Once the author sat on the rim of a valley in a northeastern state for several hours, listening to a buck blow and snort in obvious suspicion. He knew something was near which he didn't want in his domain, but as no movement occurred to drive him away, he just couldn't make up his mind what this "something" might be. There wasn't a chance in those nervous hours for an open shot; indeed only the blowing and occasional stamping of his feet confirmed the fact that a buck was down there waiting.

155

Charles Varney, right, of Turner, Maine, drags out a small buck. He has a dairy farm there with a shooting area for sportsmen.

Two beech sticks lay on the ground beside the hunter's stand. Time was passing, and further delay would eliminate a shot anyway. Finally the author picked up the sticks and cracked them together, trying to produce a rattling noise. There was a sudden silence in the valley. In about five minutes another rattle was made, and this time the snorting and blowing was nearer!

Another wait, and the final chattering was easier—the hunter's hands were trembling in excitement.

Suddenly there was a loud crash in the brush, and a huge whitetail leaped over a blowdown, going away broadside. He had found out too late what it was on the knoll that had puzzled him. Still, the author is not completely convinced this would work again.

One thing it does prove, perhaps—a man can use his reason to at least try to outwit a crafty whitetail. No sensible man would try to walk up a deer when the season is so dry that each step is like that of a crashing moose. Yet, if he has companions on stands, the noise may even be helpful! A lone hunter stalks *quietly*, taking one step backward for every one ahead, in the phraseology of experienced deer seekers. This absurdity, of course, would get him nowhere, but it should be interpreted as a classic quotation: "Make haste slowly."

In summation, then, the individual who shoots a whitetail fall after fall generally is the man who prepares his campaign ahead by seeking his buck where the food is most abundant, where the cover is good enough to "house" deer, where the terrain allows the shooter at least a minimum opportunity to match his skill against a whitetail's stealth.

Whether stalking, sitting, driving—or a combination of methods is used—may frequently depend on weather, time of year, and the number of hunters in a party. Rifles, shotguns—even hunting bows—will be used by the deer seeker according to his own preference, his skill, and hunting regulations.

Finally, it is easy enough to pile deer knee-deep in a camp or living room, but when the conversation palls and the final showdown comes, it's the man who hunts hardest, longest, and the most patiently who scores with such consistency that he can nod "Yes" when asked:

"Got your deer yet, Charlie?"

158   Charley Niehuis.

Chapter Thirteen

MULE DEER

by CHARLEY NIEHUIS

CHARLEY NIEHUIS lives in Montrose, Colorado, and doesn't have to travel too far to reach good mule-deer territory. He has done public-relations work, editing, and held positions in the Arizona Game and Fish Commission. In between he has done free-lance writing and photography, and his articles and stories have appeared in all of the outdoor magazines. At the present time he is the news bureau manager for *The Daily Sentinel,* which is published in Grand Junction, Colorado. He has also written three juvenile books called *Trapping the Silver Beaver, Steel Dust,* and *Beegee.* These are all based upon actual experiences in the out of doors.

B IG buck mule deer of the Southwest get big by being smart. As a matter of fact they have to be smart just to stay alive. A buck is usually born as a twin fawn. This is nature's insurance policy, which makes it more likely that one will manage to live and help perpetuate the species. For usually disease, shortage of food, and predation by coyotes, wildcats, mountain lions—the natural selection of only the fittest—will take one of the twins.

If the young buck is lucky and hardy and strong, then he will throw off disease and survive the hard winters. If he is fleet, he will outrun the coyote. If he stays alert, he will never be caught off guard by a stalking wildcat or mountain lion.

In short, if he has the makings of a good buck, a trophy animal, he will stay alive until the moment you outsmart him and settle your sights on him and pull the trigger.

But—to outsmart him you have to know more about the factors which have gone into making that buck big, a trophy buck.

One of the best mule-deer trophy hunters I know works all year to sharpen his own senses and abilities for that flashing instant when a big buck appears, or flushes, in front of him. H. E. "Buster" Gubernator of San Antonio, Texas, is a "head-hunter," and a good one. But he got that way only by honing certain potentialities to a keen edge.

Buster is thoroughly familiar with his rifle. He shoots month in and month out. He shoots at targets, he hunts jack rabbits and varmints. Buster, in my opinion, is almost flawless in the handling of his rifle, bringing it to his shoulder and getting a sight on a deer; and this is as it must be. A trophy mulie will give you only a fraction of a second to make up your mind about whether or not you are going to take him.

This head-hunting friend of mine is a superb shot with any of his rifles: the .270, the .30/06, or the Magnum. When he arrives— after driving 1500 miles from "San Antone"—on the Kaibab, or on the Vermilion Cliffs, or on the Arizona Strip in northern Arizona, or on Log Hill or the Uncompahgre Plateau in southwestern Colorado, that hunting rifle is as much a part of him as the forefinger on his right hand. And he can shoot the gun accurately. Accurately—heck, he is deadly with it!

Like many another buck hunter who is really good, Buster knows his hunting territory so well he can travel over it at night.

If you live near enough, do as Buster and other repeat buckgetters do. Go out on a weekend to your favorite hunting area and walk over the terrain. It will do three things: help you become familiar with the lay of the land, keep you in better physical condition for deer hunting, and give you a chance to learn something about the mule deer.

What if you can't actually get on the ground? The best alternative I know is to get a topographical map of the area. These maps can be obtained from the U. S. Forest Service, the Bureau of Land Management or the game department of the state in which you intend to hunt this fall.

A couple of letters to operators of hunting camps or resorts will get you additional information. Membership in a hunter's club or a gun club may gain you a new friend or two who know something about the territory, or have hunted there.

Add to this knowledge by going to the outdoor magazines and hunting yearbooks for articles about the particular area. Back

H. E. "Buster" Gubernator of San Antonio, Texas, with a trophy mule-deer buck taken in Arizona's Kaibab country.

files of these are usually maintained by your public library. If not, one of your new-found friends in the hunting or gun club may have a stack of back issues.

Study these in the evenings—and plan your hunt for mulies. Your planning ahead will go a long way toward getting you a buck.

But no matter how you improve your knowledge of the hunting terrain, the techniques and the habits of the quarry, you can't afford to forget for a minute that you will have to outsmart the mule-deer buck that got big and became a trophy by being smart, himself. Buster was one hunter who never forgot, I learned one fall in northern Arizona.

Rocky Mountain mule deer range throughout the western portion of the North American continent, and Kaibab Mountain, on the north side of the Grand Canyon in northern Arizona, is one of the very finest mule-deer ranges in the entire country. It has just the right elevation, rising from 4000 to a little over 8000 feet. It has the right kinds of vegetation, growing in a predominantly limestone formation. Because of this, the Kaibab has produced unique and distinctive mule-deer trophies. And consequently this area is heavily hunted. This has been true since the early pioneering days of the West, when the Kaibab, known then as Buckskin Mountain, was the scene of annual gatherings of Navajo, Ute, and Hopi Indians, for purposes of palaver and trading of artifacts for buckskins.

One fall when Buster Gubernator and I were there, 2500 hunters had permits to take a Kaibab deer. It was an Indian-summer fall, shirt-sleeve weather. Car and jeeploads of hunters were making race tracks out of the trails penetrating the ridges leading off the mountain.

We had hunted two days of a fourteen-day season and were beginning to get discouraged. At least, I was.

"Makes a fellow want to go off and hide until this rat race is over," I said morosely to Buster.

Buster turned his head and looked very solemnly at me a moment; his gray eyes shot with streaks of brown were as expressionless as the ripening berries on the manzanita bushes. Then he nodded.

Mule deer are usually found in open, high-elevation country and are shot at fairly long ranges. This is the edge of Sowats Canyon, north rim of the Grand Canyon.

"That's just what they would do," he said.

"Who?"

"Those big bucks. They'd go off in some deep canyon or way out on a point somewhere—a place that is hard to get to."

That night we studied a topographical map of the north rim of the Grand Canyon, which borders Kaibab Mountain on the south. And the next morning we were picking our way off into Sowats Canyon.

Maybe the other 2498 hunters were content to mill around together on top of the mountain, but two of us were going down into Sowats at daylight because one of us could think like a deer.

Ordinarily early in the season you'll find the bigger mule-deer bucks high in the country among the spruce and aspen. There the nights are cool and the days are bright and sunny. In early October a buck is hardening and polishing his antlers. He'll try to lie in the shade, with his antlers in the sun. He'll walk in close to a group of aspen saplings, or a stand of jack pines, and rake them with his antlers, sharpening and polishing the tines.

He'll be with other big bucks of his kind.

Yearling bucks and two-year-olds will most often be running with Mama at a lower elevation.

Then when the storms and snows come to the uplands, such as the 8000-foot-high Kaibab Plateau, the big bucks drift down into lower country to the winter ranges. Thus the big bucks and the does come together in November for the rut, or mating.

It is now that the sharpened tines and polished antlers come into play, during the fight for supremacy of the harem of does a big mule deer collects and guards.

But that year on the Kaibab, though the weather was mild, it was an unusual situation. The horde of hunters was causing the big bucks to migrate early to the more inaccessible lower country, such as Sowats Canyon, and out onto the Fishtail—so Buster reasoned.

Buster and I said some last words to each other at breakfast, for down in Sowats we didn't speak. We walked slowly, stopping frequently, looking, listening—and not talking.

Sowats is a big canyon. Sheer escarpments form the rim. Snow, rain, ice, and heat have broken the rimrocks and caused long, steep talus slopes to form into the canyon.

Shoulder- and head-high brush cover the flat canyon bottom, and this blocked our view ahead. So we climbed up on the side in order to see ahead and down into the bottom.

Buster was in the lead when the buck flushed. That mulie bounded into sight, clearing a six-foot-high wall of manzanita. And with a silk-smooth movement Buster had his rifle to his shoulder, following the flight of the buck.

The deer slid around a bush, disappeared. Came into sight again. Tucked his forelegs back, vaulting into the air to skim over a boulder.

He never straightened out those front legs. Buster's well-aimed .270 smashed his backbone in mid-flight.

Three things had made that hunt pay off: first, reasoning where a big buck that was concerned with staying alive might be; secondly, studying a topographical map to locate a likely place to hunt; and finally, shooting skill when the target presented itself.

Sometimes knowledge of two other factors will help in hunting mule deer. The Kaibab, because of its unique formation and outstanding deer herd, has been a study area for those interested in wildlife management.

I once sat in a session with a group of wildlife experts, and as a hunter I asked the question, "What, in your opinion, contributes most to a successful hunt?"

One of the wildlife men replied, "Knowing what a mule deer eats, and knowing where quantities of such forage are to be found."

A mule deer is a browsing animal. Watch one sometime. It nibbles at the twigs of bushes, nips off a bit of weed, takes a step or two and takes a bite of something else. Stomach analyses of deer show the variety of vegetation they eat: quinine bush is a prime favorite on the Kaibab. Aspen leaves from tiny saplings, new growth of sage, mushrooms, acorns, a trace of grass, weeds, all are taken into a deer's paunch when it is feeding, to be regurgitated and chewed as a cud when it is resting.

A deer ranges forth two times a day, under normal circumstances, and eats approximately ten pounds of forage. This happens at daylight and again at dusk. It takes a buck two to four hours to fill his belly, the time varying according to the amount of forage available, of course.

A smart buck mule-deer hunter on the Kaibab takes this into consideration. He first finds areas of quinine brush, then hunts in this area during the very early hours and again just before nightfall.

After 9 A.M. and until two hours before sunset our smart hunter will hunt the areas where deer would be bedding down, sleeping, and chewing their cud.

And where does a deer bed down? A buck that is big enough

and smart enough to know the ways of a life where danger is constant?

On a bright, warm, sunshiny day, when the flies and gnats are annoying, a buck will lie on the point of a ridge that is swept by a prevailing breeze. The wind, slight as it may be, will do two things for the buck; blow the stinging flies and gnats away and bring to the buck any scent of danger.

Usually he will lie in his bed so situated that he can see his back trail, because it's nine to one he traveled upwind a hundred yards before he bedded down.

If you hunt upwind, move slowly and as quietly as possible, in order to avoid flushing your buck before you get close enough to get a shot. You will have to stop and look often, if you want to see him before he sees you.

The ability to see a buck in his bed really takes practice. You've got to know where to look, and even then all too often you overlook him, since he can hold completely still and is well camouflaged by hornlike branches and deer-colored earth and rocks.

On a hot day a buck will usually lie in the shade of a bush, tree, rock, or deadfall, in the path of a cooling breeze. This will often be out on a point or shoulder of land just below the crest.

Being out on a point will give him several routes of escape, should be need them: either way around the point down into the canyon or back over the ridge.

And on a hot day he will flush sooner than on a cold one. For if the day is gusty, with the weather on the verge of storming, perhaps the sky breaking to let patches of warming sunlight through now and then, the buck will seek a shelter from the cold wind, yet a place exposed to the sun. If he has a comfortable spot he will be either reluctant to leave or so snug and cozy he allows his senses to relax their vigilance a bit.

So, on a bright, hot day the west slope of a ridge is the place to go looking for bucks in the morning. On a cold, blustery day, hunt the places you would seek out if you were going to lie down and keep warm.

Actually, a buck deer is a creature of comfort and a home lover. If food, water, and shelter are available, a buck will stay within a two- to three-mile area until some outside force causes him to move.

Should the water hole dry up and forage become scant, he will drift. A prowling mountain lion will cause him to change his range. A stream of hunters that must be avoided will make him migrate. Severe winter storms and the rutting season will move him to seek another area.

Mule Deer

But unless something does nudge him out of his home range, you will find the same mule deer in the same general area year after year. For this reason he gets to know it as you know the pattern of the creases in the palm of your hand. He knows every escape route, every thicket, all the bed grounds, and where the choicest forage is to be found. His range is his home. So, to get him, you must know his stamping ground as well as he does, and that's not easy.

But—it is of just such things that expertise is made. And this is what makes hunting for a trophy buck Rocky Mountain mule deer such great sport.

168   Dr. Ray Bentzen.

Chapter Fourteen

PRONGHORN ANTELOPE

by DR. RAY BENTZEN

DR. RAY BENTZEN practiced dentistry for thirty-three years in Sheridan, Wyoming, where he was born. In 1962 he retired and moved to a tree farm near Umpqua, Oregon. He has specialized in big-game hunting for many species in the western states, Canada, and Alaska. He has held several records for antelope, mule deer, elk, and grizzly bear and has won many awards in rifle and shotgun shooting. In addition to his outdoor hobbies he also goes in for horticulture, exploring, archaeology, and woodworking. His articles have appeared in professional and outdoor magazines.

M ANY years ago, while hunting alone, I saw a herd of about thirty antelope browsing on a long bench of land which was bordered on one side by a ridge and on the other by an arroyo about eight feet deep. Although they were half a mile away, my binoculars revealed that the single buck present had an extremely wide spread of horns, more so than I ever had seen before.

There was little or no breeze, and my car was on the opposite side of the arroyo from them. The antelope were watching me, so I drove the car in the opposite direction from them until I reached a point where I could slip out of the car and into the arroyo without their seeing me. The buck had been standing a little apart from and on the far side of the herd of does and fawns. Fortunately, the arroyo was deep enough so that I could walk upright the entire distance, which I did until I was slightly beyond the spot where the antelope had been.

After recovering my breath, I picked out a large sagebrush on the edge of the arroyo, and, removing my hat, I peeked through the brush. The animals had moved very little. The herd was to my left and the big buck slightly out to the right, about 250 yards away. I brought the rifle up very carefully, pushed the barrel through the sagebrush, settled the sight just back of the shoulder, and dropped the buck with a clean heart shot. His horns, although not overly large, had a spread of 19½ inches, which at that time was second to the world's record.

The pronghorn antelope (*Antilocapra americana*) is a strange animal without a close relative. He has horns like a goat or sheep, but he sheds them late every year, leaving a bony core exposed over which the new horny sheath will develop the following year. The horns are jet-black like a goat's, lyre-shaped with the points usually turned in, and have a prong on the front edge. The antelope is the only North American mammal that sheds its horns annually.

Unlike other game animals, which have protective coloration, the antelope is extremely conspicuous in his native habitat, the western plains. He is predominately tan on the upper neck, sides, and back, while the lower neck, brisket, sides, and rump patch are snow-white. The nose and upper face are dark on the does, black on the bucks. The black face of a buck can often be seen at a greater distance than his horns, a good sex determiner. When aroused, the antelope raises the snow-white hairs of his rump patch so that it resembles a pillow and can easily be seen for a mile.

Antelope are the easiest to locate of all big-game animals because of their conspicuous coloring and the open country in which they live, but they are one of the most difficult to approach, because of their wariness and extremely good eyesight. It has been stated that an antelope's eyes are equal to 8-power binoculars, and I believe that is true. Their eyes are positioned in such a manner that they can see backward as well as forward, and if a person pokes his head up over a ridge as much as half a mile away, a feeding antelope will most always erect his head for a better look at the intruder. This characteristic makes them most difficult to stalk and explains why so many poor sportsmen prefer the illegal method of using a car to run them down.

An average mature buck antelope in Wyoming will weigh

The pronghorn antelope is wary, has extremely good eyesight, and is one of the fastest big-game animals in North America. (*South Dakota Dept. of Game, Fish and Parks photo*)

90 to 100 pounds field-dressed, or 70 pounds quartered. Some observers say that Oregon and Arizona antelope are slightly larger, while those in Mexico are smaller. This variation could be attributed to available forage. The antelope is primarily a browsing animal, preferring shrubs and weeds rather than grasses. In the big blizzard winter of 1948–49, on the Barlow ranches in Campbell County, Wyoming, the forage had been so denuded by grasshoppers the summer before that nothing was left but beds of cactus, yet 500 head of antelope wintered without any perceptible loss on a diet of cactus pods, breaking open the pods with their sharp hoofs to avoid the sharp thorns!

The national antelope population swung from many millions in the 1800s down to a low of 27,000 in 1923, and now they have increased to the point where Wyoming issues 45,000 permits a year, and many more than that are killed each season. Like sheep, they breed at an early age and usually have twins, so the herds build rapidly and stand much shooting pressure.

Antelope country is usually rolling, hilly country with washes and arroyos. This gives the hunter a chance to approach them by keeping out of sight in an arroyo or behind a hill until within range, which may well be 300 or 400 yards. Close shots on antelope are rare. Of the more than half a hundred buck antelope which I have killed, the ones which were shot at less than 200 yards could be counted on your fingers. For this reason, use a gun with flat trajectory and great accuracy. My own favorite, which I use on everything including Canadian moose and Alaskan brown bear, is the 300 Weatherby Magnum and hand loads using 180-grain Core-lokt bullets and 79 grains of 4350 powder, a maximum load. With this load sighted in for zero at 200 yards, the dot reticle can be rested on top of the antelope's shoulder at 400 yards and will kill every time. A standing shot can usually be had at that distance, unless the buck is extremely wary, or in the event of a cold, windy day, when the animals are always spooky. In warm or calm weather the animals prefer the ridges and slopes, alternating between browsing and reclining, but in hot, sultry, or windy weather, they prefer the cool, quiet floors of arroyos or canyons to rest or browse.

No other animal, pound for pound, can take the punishment

of a rifle bullet like an antelope. He is the toughest of all. The only shot that will anchor him for sure is a brain or spine shot. The first antelope I ever killed had part of his heart and a big segment of lung tissue torn out with a .30/06 bullet, yet he ran fifteen yards, ducked under a fence, ran a twenty-yard circle, ducked under the fence again, and then traveled another fifteen yards before dropping. I have seen antelope, on several occasions, go a quarter of a mile or more, dragging their stomach and intestines on the ground, after a bullet had ripped open their bellies. That is why I like to be "overgunned." The more shocking power a bullet delivers, the less apt an animal is to get away.

Pronghorn Antelope

One season I knew there were many fine heads in the Pumpkin Butte area of Wyoming, so I arranged for a government hunter friend to accompany me, and we went there the day before the season opened and glassed heads all day, about sixty of them. We saw many better than average, but none big enough for Boone & Crockett competition. The next day we started in again at daylight, and by nine o'clock had located a real trophy head. A careful stalk was planned and executed, and in another hour I was the proud possessor of a magnificent head which I had killed with a single shot at 370 steps. The horns were 16¾ inches long, had a 17⅝-inch spread, and were symmetrical and heavy. The head measured larger than the seven previous national champions, but it was my tough luck that three larger heads were entered that same year. Incidentally, the pronghorn which took second place that year was killed by a friend of mine who had never before been antelope hunting and who was interested only in the meat, but this monster nearly ran over him, so he shot it and then had to be coaxed to enter the head in the national competition.

The antelope is the most fleet-footed of any North American big-game animal. He can course along easily at 50 miles per hour, and on several occasions I have had a buck run parallel to and even with my car on a straight country lane at 55 miles per hour for half a mile or more, and then, seeming to want to prove his superiority, suddenly put on a burst of speed that would take him across the lane in front of the car, which would require a speed of at least 60 miles per hour. The normal running speed of the antelope, however, is from 30 to 50 miles per hour.

His gait is a poetry of motion. Unlike the deer, which uses a bounding motion, the antelope glides along with his body on a smooth, even keel, his lightning-fast legs taking up all the unevenness between body and terrain. He cannot, or at least does not, jump. Most of the wire fences in antelope country are either three or four strands of barbed wire, or four-foot woven wire, and in all my years of hunting I have never seen an antelope jump over a fence. They nearly always crawl under, but sometimes between the wires. This is often the downfall of a buck who is wary of getting his horns entangled in the wire while crawling under a fence.

I remember one site on a 20,000 acre ranch in Wyoming which I named the "coffin-corner" because of the number of buck antelope killed there. It consisted of a mile of tight, four-barb-wire fence joining another half mile at right angles. Whenever a herd of antelope or even a lone buck was spotted within the angle of the two fences, the hunter could drive the animals with his vehicle (illegal though it was) toward the angle in the fence, and although the does and fawns would crawl under and escape, the buck, fearful of getting his horns caught in the wire, would run back and forth until the hunter's bullet stopped him.

Much has been written about the natural curiosity of the antelope. I believe that this aspect has been overplayed and that much of it has been conjectural or imaginative. However, the antelope does exhibit more curiosity than other big-game animals. If a person can conceal himself, tie a white rag to a stick, and wave it gently where the animal can see it, he *may* approach to investigate it. More often he will not. Young bucks are the most curious, especially if they are alone. The does are gregarious, and in a group, as with people, there are always some more nervous than the others. These nervous ones will spook and run at the slightest pretext, and the gang goes along. Personally, I have never been able to lure a trophy buck within range by waving a white flag, but I do not doubt that many others have done so.

The antelope depends on his powerful eyes to warn him of

danger and on his speedy legs to take him away to safety. As a general rule, scent and sound can be disregarded, or at least minimized, when hunting antelope, because of the distance involved. Of course, human voices and the sound of a motor will put them to flight, especially after they have been coursed or shot at.

Antelope are completely unpredictable. When startled, they may start running in one direction, then suddenly reverse themselves and take the opposite direction. I have crossed the top of a roundish knoll, surprised an antelope on the opposite side, and then had him run in a complete circle around me at 50 yards' distance before taking off in another direction. I have also had them run to within forty feet of me on open prairie before veering off to one side.

More ammunition is wasted in hunting antelope than with any other big game. This is due mainly to the speed of the target and partly to the small size of the animal. I have known of several instances where novices have fired as many as four boxes of cartridges, eighty rounds, without killing their antelope. The antelope runs so smoothly that his speed is unbelievable, and the inexperienced hunter will always shoot behind the target. Let us do a little figuring. Take an antelope running broadside at 50 miles per hour. He is traveling at the rate of 73 feet per second. A standard .30/06 rifle bullet at 2700 feet per second will require .22 seconds to travel 200 yards. In that length of time the antelope has covered 16 feet or 4 body lengths. At 200 yards distance, with the animal running broadside at full speed, it is necessary that the rifle sight be pointed 16 feet or 4 body lengths ahead of the target at the moment of trigger-squeeze. Once a person realizes these facts, he'll start making hits instead of raising the dust behind the animals.

A rancher friend of mine, Glenn Barlow, taught me a method of meat preparation on antelope (which works equally well on deer) that beats anything I ever heard of. First, kill a nice two-year-old buck with a neck shot. The two-year-olds are usually off by themselves and are inexperienced enough to allow the hunter to approach close enough for a neck shot. With a sharp knife, rip the skin only from the vent to the chin, leaving the

175

Henry P. Boos of Minneapolis, a highly skilled shot on running game, with an antelope killed in Wyoming.

belly unopened. Skin one side of the entire animal to a point just beyond the spine. Spread the detached skin on the ground and roll the carcass over on it. Skin the other side. Cut off the head and feet. Spread a clean cloth or canvas in your car. Remove the hams completely at the ball-and-socket joint, taking all the meat to the pelvic bone, and lay them on the clean cloth. Detach both shoulders from the ribs and lay them on the cloth. Insert the knife parallel to the spinal bones and separate the backstrap or loin from the spine the full length of the carcass on each side of the spine. Place the knife parallel to the ribs and separate the loin from the ribs clear to the pelvis. Put the loins on the cloth. Now 95 per cent of the meat is detached from the body, and the abdominal and chest cavities have not even been opened. This insures no contamination of chest or belly contents with the meat, and no blood. If the heart and liver are desired, it is a simple matter to open the belly and remove them.

Here is another hint that is wonderful. Butchers always cut round steaks off the ham in a single plane. This means that part of each steak is tough because it is cut with the grain instead of at right angles to it. The hind quarter or ham is composed of three main muscles which are not all parallel to each other. Using a sharp knife, separate these three main muscles from the bone and tendons. There will be two long, slender ones and one short, thick one. Now cut steaks off each one at right angles to the grain, the same as pork chops. This also eliminates any bone-sawing. You'll find that the meat will be much more tender than ordinary round steak.

A number of years ago I was guiding a party consisting of Dr. and Mrs. Wynn Beebe, of Seattle, and Dr. and Mrs. Marvin Beebe, of Hamilton, Montana, on their first antelope hunt, in Campbell County, Wyoming. All four of them were successful in killing their antelope, although it took a number of shots, it being their first experience. Then I told them we would search for a trophy head for myself, so we drove the Dodge power wagon around the hills and plains for another hour till we spotted a trophy buck and a doe walking slowly over the crest of a hill about half a mile away. When they were out of sight, I drove swiftly to the spot where they disappeared, expecting to see them within easy range, but they must have seen or heard us coming, because they were hightailing it across a big swale, way out of range.

On an impulse, I decided to chance a long shot, so I took the Magnum, threw myself to the ground in a prone position, aimed at a point about fifteen feet above and thirty feet to the left of the quartering buck, and squeezed off the trigger. To the great surprise of all of us, the buck went down, an instant kill. The fellows yelled like Comanche Indians, and Mary was so elated that she kissed me. Marvin insisted on stepping off the distance. He is six feet two inches tall. I checked the speedometer on the power wagon and the rest of us drove in a straight line to the buck. The speedometer registered exactly half a mile! When I finished dressing the buck, Marvin strode up and announced, "Guess what—880 steps!" It was the longest running shot I ever made, and I never expect to duplicate it, but it brings wonderful memories.

Chapter Fifteen

ELK HUNTING
by CLYDE ORMOND

CLYDE ORMOND was born in the Upper Snake River Valley, near Rigby, Idaho, the town where he still lives. He's had a varied background which embraces playing in dance bands, boxing, inventing, art, and teaching. He was both a teacher and principal in two school systems for twelve years. He started writing professionally in 1938 and now estimates he has had over two million words published. This includes six books, a newspaper column, and numerous articles in the outdoor and gun magazines. This writing has taken him to the better hunting country from Mexico to the Arctic. At the present time he is a contributing editor to *American Rifleman* magazine. One of his more popular books is *Hunting Our Biggest Game*.

LAST fall in the high mountains of western Wyoming, and about six hard miles from Glidden McNeel's camp, the guide and I located a small band of elk. They were picked up with 9-power binoculars across a mile-wide basin, appearing as but small tan specks as they grazed out of the shadows in the late afternoon just under a craggy peak.

It was too late and too far to go after them, so we returned to camp without disclosing our presence.

The next morning before frosty daylight, we'd left camp. By full sunup we'd reached the near side of the basin. Hiding the saddle horses in a clump of pines, we sat concealed and began bugling across the shadow-filled basin on an artificial bamboo elk bugle, toward where the elk band had been.

About the second toot, the distant, high-pitched squeal of a maddened bull elk, who thought his harem of cows was about to be invaded by another bull, came echoing back, "Da-da-da-daeeeee-da-dan-dum . . . grunt, grunt!"

The small band had moved part way down the opposite side

179

180   Clyde Ormond.

of the basin. By the second time the bull challenged, we had him marked down.

Within the hour, we had circled the basin head out of sight with the horses. Three hundred yards from the alternate thick pines and open alps where the bull had been marked down, we climbed noiselessly from the horses, and I took off, pussyfooting through the heavy blowdown timber on foot. Two hundred yards later, as I strained my eyes to catch sight of him across a tiny open alp where I knew he must be, the big herd bull spooked. He'd been watching, concealed all but his heavy antlers, in second-growth pines, and had caught my scent or some faint sound.

Four shots (one a complete miss) from the Remington 7-mm Magnum, using 175-grain bullets, had the bull's "horseshoes" in the air before he could race off into the thick timber . . .

An analysis of this simple incident will disclose a wealth of vital and basic elk-hunting lore. In fact, every aspect of that episode has a direct bearing on the technique of hunting elk in wilderness country.

First, elk, once plains animals, now inhabit the remaining high, remote, and wilderness areas. There they remain in hunting season and only come down with heavy snow and the threat to their food supply. Again, the great animals are spooky to a high degree, wary of man, and cannot, as can deer, live in close proximity to human beings. Further, during the mating season, or rut, the sexes band together. The bulls will "bugle" and can be made to answer a properly blown artificial call, simulating the actual calling, or bugling, of the wild bulls.

Of equal importance to the hunter are the facts that a spooked elk, once he has figured things out and has made up his mind, is apt to head in a straight line for a distant basin and never stop for five miles or more; that the hunting camp must be placed far enough away from where the game is expected to be, so as not to have any camp noises disclose its presence; and that the ideal way of cutting down the necessary mountain distances between such a camp and where the game is found, is by horseback.

Lastly, and equally fundamental to successful elk hunting, are the facts that a spooked or moving elk watches his back track, lays down a retreat pattern that is hard to follow without revealing the hunter's presence, and offers only a hind-end shot; and it takes a lot of horsepower in the cartridge to down him cleanly.

Once these basic factors are understood, the hunter is in a position to outwit the quarry in its own timbered bailiwick.

In a broad way, the remaining elk are distributed over a mountainous belt of country coincident with the Rocky Mountains and from New Mexico to Alberta, Canada; in the provinces of Saskatchewan and Manitoba; in coastal areas overlapping the states of Oregon-California, Oregon-Washington; and on Vancouver Island off the coast of Washington.

The hunter's best chance for elk is where the concentrations are greatest and where hunting pressure is least. The very best elk hunting today is in primitive country, reached by pack and saddle stock.

The actual techniques of elk hunting are of several types, which often overlap. The simplest form of elk hunting is stalking. In this, the hunter makes his camp a mile or so from where the game is expected to be and strikes off on foot. The best period of the day for this kind of hunting is the dawn-to-sunup period. Elk move most at this hour, are found more in the open and "edge" areas (where timber meets open alps), and during the rut will bugle more at this period. All this helps to reveal their presence. The second-best period is from sundown-till-dark.

In stalking, it is a cardinal rule that one must go much slower than he thinks necessary. Stationary and alert game picks up movement easily. The stationary or slow-moving hunter can detect moving game far more easily than if he moves fast.

As with other species of game, the hunter should "work" the ridges and endeavor to go high so as to hunt downward on his quarry. Game has been conditioned by the necessities of survival into watching for its enemies from below; and all game may be approached closer from above.

In stalking up ridges, the hunter is apt to locate elk as they themselves are feeding on or moving along the mountain spines. Elk like ridges because from them they can see in four directions and have a handy retreat pattern available in all four. Also, in early morning elk will feed from ridge cover onto the sunny

A cow and bull elk, spooked, leaving the area in a hurry.

sides of the hill at daylight, then move back into the shadows of the northern slopes for shading up for the day. This habit, and the time of morning, give a clue to the hunter as to where the game may currently be found.

Usually by nine o'clock, in wilderness country, elk will shade up for the day and be found in the heaviest thickets and blowdown. This is an escape strategy—heavy timber cannot be negotiated by an enemy (man) without noise to disclose a pursuer's presence.

Canyon and basin apexes are fine places to stalk and glass. From such an apex both sides of a basin may be studied, and often standing or bedded elk can be picked up with binoculars. Once game is located, the successful technique for making the final stalk is in some way, to approach the game from an unsuspected direction. That is, elk will normally watch their back tracks and look for pursuers coming up from below as they pause or rest just under some timbered crest, or near the apex of a high mountain basin or saddle. The hunter must, by utilizing the terrain and foliage to conceal him, come upon such game from behind and just over the *opposing* ridge. He must work against any wind or breeze in doing this, otherwise the elk will catch his scent. Again, such a final stalk often entails the circling of a half mile or more in order to gain a few hundred yards of distance. But the key factor is to approach from an unsuspected direction.

Tracks and dung help the stalker. The tracks of a bull elk are about four inches across, roundish in contour (like a big, split coffee cup), and will show dew-claw imprints in mud. Dung is in kernel form, dark, elliptical in shape, and looks like almonds.

Both dung and spoor identify the species, and by their freshness help to indicate the proximity to game.

I have found that it is a poor technique for the stalker to try to "track game down." This is because game watches its back track, and plans a campaign of moving in such a way that pursuers can always be located along such a back track by having to cross openings, or noisy foliage. The game watches and listens for these giveaways.

A far more productive technique for the stalker is to generally parallel a fresh track from above and watch for the game below; or to circle so as to come upon the quarry in some area to which it is apparently headed.

One big disadvantage in trying to track game down is that any shot the hunter may get is at the elk's rear end. Hind-end shots won't kill elk even with the most powerful cartridges.

The careful stalker uses his senses of sight, smell, and hearing to detect the game's presence. Elk in timber don't usually show up as *elk*. They are dark or tan spots which don't belong; an inverted "horseshoe" of tan, which is an elk's rump; a longitudinal line or silhouette (the animal's back) upon a sky line; a tiny letter T above foliage (cow's head and uplifted ears); or lines and shapes which are inharmonious with the surroundings, but which, upon close scrutiny, resolve into the form of a partially concealed animal.

In heavy timber, and at distances under a hundred yards, elk can often be smelled—this, from the sweetish, musky odor of fresh urine. The instant a hunter smells this, he should make ready for a quick shot. Again, the mild crackings of twigs and chattering up ahead may mean squirrels. It may also mean elk feeding and that the squirrels have discovered them or the hunter. The literal "bark," as from a small dog, means to the experienced hunter that a cow elk has detected his presence and is warning her calf of danger.

Stalking elk in snow is similar to stalking over dry terrain, except that the tracks tell a clear story. The same techniques should be used—circle the spoor to come upon game from above, parallel any tracks instead of following them, move more slowly than appears necessary, work into any breeze, not with it, and utilize any differences in terrain so as to remain concealed from view but to come upon the quarry from an unsuspected direction.

A thrilling and successful technique is to hunt on saddle horses. This is the means often employed in remote country where distances are great, and pack stock are necessary in conjunction, to pack in the meat quarters. Most big outfitters supply horses for elk hunting.

The basic habits of elk remain the same, but the use of riding horses, while permitting far greater distances to be covered, often necessitates a change in the hunting procedure. Briefly, horses in most wilderness country have to graze at night to keep well-fed. Hay transportation is too great a problem. This entails wrangling the horses in the morning, which takes time. This, plus the fact that the base camp must be placed far enough from expected game so as not to spook it, makes it difficult to be where the game is by that best period of the day, daybreak-till-sunup.

Only where some horse feed is available at camp, or where a couple of horses especially needed are fed oats and tied overnight, as was done in the instance mentioned earlier, can the daybreak hunting be taken advantage of.

Hunting from horses is comparable to foot stalking. The high ridges are ridden with as little noise and talking as possible. Intervening canyons, basins, and gully apexes are studied and glassed with binoculars. Seven to 9-power binoculars are fine for this, and a light spotting-scope and tripod carried in the saddlebags are worth their weight for scrutinizing game and country at long range. Glassing is done from all available promontories; bluffs, and high points overlooking big or lower country. While glassing for game, the hunter should constantly keep his ear peeled for the bugle of the bulls, which is equally useful in locating the animals.

Once game is located, the horses are ridden only close enough to avoid too much walking but always out of sight. The horses are then tied securely out of sight, and the final stalk to within shooting distances is made on foot. In tying horses, incidentally, a horse should be tied even with his nose when in normal standing position, leaving approximately four feet of rope between animal and tree. Novices who simply drop the reins of many hunting horses find themselves with a long walk back to camp.

After the early morning hunting, two techniques often pay off in horseback hunting elk in timber. One is simply to ride noiselessly through belts of timber where fresh elk spoor is visible or game may be logically expected and watch the horse. Mountain horses experienced in hunting will often pause while walking, cock their heads to one side, stop, and stand with ears pointed forward. I've located many an elk by aiming straight

Resting during midday for lunch at a high lake. Most elk country requires the use of horses to cover the necessary distances.

with the eyes down between the alerted nag's ears. The sight of game has caused the animal to stop and look.

Again, after elk have shaded up or bedded down for the day in thick timber, a hunter can make the situation pay off if he has a partner or is hunting with a guide. Briefly, the horses are tied out of sight (usually just over the next crest), and the hunter is posted at the *upper* end of the timber belt, in such a position that he can view some sort of opening. The partner then circles the patch of timber silently and comes up through it from the lower end, making no move to keep quiet or out of sight. If elk are in that patch of timber, they will move out, and habitually up through to the apex, where the posted hunter gets his chance.

The technique is useful not only for small timber patches where elk are thought to be, but for entire canyons, small basins, and gully heads. Several hunters are more useful than just two for big canyons. Often one of the hunters pushing up from below will get a shot before the game is alerted and moves upward.

Generally, in horseback hunting, the middle of the day will be least productive. Where long distances from camp must be covered, the most successful period of the day will be at dusk. Elk will move again after the shadows begin to lengthen in the canyons and will gradually feed out into open alps, small parks, and edge areas. A trick which the veteran elk hunter has learned is that elk will normally move just *inside* the camouflage of these lengthening shadows—not out in the open sunlight. Keen scrutiny is necessary to locate them in such shadow.

The use of horses makes it possible to cover a lot of country and study many such likely areas. When game is located, the horses are tied and left, and the final stalking done on foot. Even in instances when one may ride virtually up on elk, no shooting should *ever* be done off the riding horse. It's too unsteady, it's inhumane, to blast away between Dobbin's ears, and in most cases the hunter will find himself high up in the sky immediately afterward, then picking up handfuls of gravel as the nag lopes off for camp.

Of all the sporting and thrilling ways to hunt elk, bugling for the bulls during mating season is tops. There is no more exciting form of hunting.

Briefly, the bulls during the rut will answer an artificial call, or bugle, if it is blown correctly and with judgment. To them it is the challenge of another bull who means to invade the harem of cows, and the answering call is a challenge to battle.

I have successfully "bugled up" elk for decades, both for myself and for hunting partners. In that time, I have only found one material from which a bugle with a true tone can be made. That's node-free bamboo. The artificial bugle I now use was made, after several not-quite-perfect attempts, from a piece of node-free bamboo seventeen-inches long, and nearly one inch in diameter. It was carved quite like an old-fashioned willow whistle Grandpa used to make, and "tuned" by carefully moving a fitted wooden plug into the blowing end until the four separate tones of the wild bull elk's bugling could be duplicated. Once in that position, the plug was glued solidly and trimmed. After years of listening to bull elk and practicing on artificial calls, I can toot on that old gas pipe and deceive almost any elk or hunter at distances of over a hundred yards. (*Note:* The author does not make the above elk bugle for sale. I have, however, included with this chapter a drawing of such a call show-

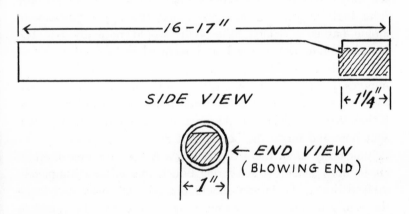

Elk bugle.
The bamboo stock is from 16 to 17 inches long by 1 inch outside diameter and of node-free bamboo. Side view shows spot to make notch, which is 1¼ inches from blowing end of bugle. The hardwood plug shown in end view is made to fit exactly inside blowing end. To "tune" the bugle, this plug is carefully adjusted back and forth inside blowing end until it just protrudes into the angular cut notch on top, or until all the four tones can be blown. When blowing, left palm is held over open end, sealing off all air. When end plug has been precisely fitted and tuned, it is cemented in place with model-airplane cement. The end plug is shaved flat on top to admit air into bugle. This flattening is done by small degrees, with trials until the tones can be blown.

ing the dimensions and giving some details of its construction.)

Other materials such as plastic hose, aluminum tubing, whistles, and even plastic commercial bugles have been used. All these lack the deep resonance of the actual bull's beller. Also, under today's hunting pressure, elk are becoming more wary—especially those which survive for several seasons. One sour toot on an artificial call will shut a bugling bull up for keeps and becomes but an aid to conservation.

Briefly, in bugling for elk an artificial call should only be used during the rutting season. It should be blown by the hunter only after he has learned the actual call of a wild bull and has practiced it at home until the sound can be duplicated.

In use, an elk bugle should only be blown at that time of day, from the particular places, and under those identical conditions under which a challenging bull elk would bugle to another bull or the herd bull of an elk band. This means to bugle only at the daybreak-sunup and sundown-dark periods; to bugle only from high ridges, canyon apexes, and the upper portions of alpine basins in which other bulls would normally be. The hunter should be concealed by foliage when he bugles.

The hunter should only bugle a single time, then wait for ten minutes. If there is no answer, he should bugle again. If no answer comes after he's bugled three times, he should move on. Either there is no bull in the area, or the hunter has blown a sour note and made the beast suspicious.

Judiciously used, the artificial bugle is the best mile-saver in elk hunting. Once the answering bull is located and completely marked down, the hunter should put the call away and make the final stalk on foot to within range. Elk cannot be called in with a bugle in the way mallards are quacked in with a call to decoys—though I have often made bulls so mad they'd fight dry trees, horn standing timber, and squeal back (at maybe 300 yards) like a maddened Hereford.

Lastly, cartridges of considerable horsepower should be used, especially for the big trophy bulls. They are mighty tough to put down and keep down, and a wounded bull in heavy timber is usually lost. Cartridges of the .300 H&H Magnum, .308 Norma, .300 Winchester Magnum, and .338 Winchester Magnum are ideal. The .30/06 and .270 class of cartridge is minimum. The lung-heart shot on elk is the best one and most easily achieved for most hunters. Relatively heavy bullets should be used.

Yes, elk hunting is a real he-man's sport. Once you've gone into primitive elk country and succeeded in bagging one on the game's own terms, you will know that you've been places and accomplished something!

A bugle properly used can make a bull elk answer and expose him for a shot.

Bradford Angier.

Chapter Sixteen

MOOSE CAN BE TOUGH

by BRADFORD ANGIER

BRADFORD ANGIER is a former newspaperman and later trade-magazine editor in Boston, who finally resigned to devote all his time to outdoor living and free-lance writing. This dream of many city dwellers was accomplished with his wife, Vena, in a log cabin in the heart of North America's best moose country—on the remote headwaters of the Peace River near Hudson Hope, British Columbia. His experiences and adventures there resulted in several popular books on wild foods, woodcraft, and other means of survival. These include *Living off the Country, How to Go Live in the Woods on $10 a Week,* and his most recent book, *We Like It Wild.*

MOOSE can be tough to nab, sure. But these days if you want one badly enough to go all out for it fairly and squarely, you're a cinch to be sitting down to some of the best eating this hemisphere has to offer. All any reasonably able hunter needs is the persistence and the time. In this air age, the best moose hunting in the world is only a few hours from any city on this continent.

What is the best time of the year to hunt North America's biggest herbivorous game animal? What are some of the most productive areas? Which moose supply the best meat when? What techniques pay off most often when you're gunning for these all-time giants of the deer family?

Let's not fool ourselves. The answers to all these questions can be considerably important. You get to see a lot of fine scenery and inhale plenty of clean air on any moose hunt. But the old bounce won't be there afterward if your only mementos are a chewed antler picked up behind a log and a snapshot of tracks, longer and slimmer than those of domestic cattle, leading off into the wild bush yonder.

If you put your cash on the line for a moose license, you want to bring home as much as you can handle of a moose you knocked over yourself. It's the answering of an instinct as old as mankind. Let people call it what they will, but each of us still kills to live; though he may hire it done by the stockyard, the tannery, or the pharmaceutical concern.

The moose is far and away the heftiest game animal in the New World that is widely hunted for its meat. Grizzly and polar bear grow bigger, it's true, but neither is noted for its steaks. Moose meat is something else again. To put it briefly, it has been my chief sustenance for many winters in the Far North, and by choice.

If moose meat is a novelty in your kitchen, here are two suggestions. Moose is apt to be rather dry, so you'll want to do what you can to keep those chops, steaks, and roasts from getting overcooked. If your moose is not well marbled with fat, try adding beef fat. Most butcher shops will sell you a bagful for a dime, and it can make all the difference.

But first you have to shoot your moose. A hundred million or so North Americans think that the only good moose hunting was back in pioneer days. They have the idea that moose have been just about shot off. That's not true by a long way. Settlement and development have resulted in moose becoming scarce in many regions, especially near and below the Canadian–U.S. border. But farther north they've actually helped the huge mammal.

British Columbia is an example. Moose were unknown in the central interior of this province until about fifty years ago. Moose then started their southward march, advancing about fifteen miles yearly. Why? Burning, logging, and otherwise clearing the dense forests created ideal range for the big animals, one of which can eat forty to fifty pounds of browse a day. It was in 1905 that moose were first sighted south of Prince George. Now they've moved down to the International Boundary. The thickest British Columbia moose populations are in this newly invaded area.

So have no doubt that a moose with your name on it isn't back of beyond or that you shouldn't take it when the decisive

A bull moose is an awesome animal with massive antlers and huge body. This close-up was taken at Harvey Lake, Alaska. (*Malcolm Greany—U. S. Fish and Wildlife Service photo*)

instant arrives. A far more valid concern? Just how are you going to connect and collect?

If there is any surer or more spine-tingling way of bagging a moose than by tracking it in fresh snow, I haven't come across it in a double decade of moose hunting from coast to coast. Older snowfall affords the next best bet. This is apt to be noisy, however, and there may be other tracks new enough to be confusing.

When you have a choice, get out before dawn after the storm has stopped. Head at a good pace in the most likely direction with a view to cutting a track by the time there's daylight enough to follow it.

Can you tell sex by tracks? Yes, to some extent. A bull, especially one of trophy proportions, will keep to more open going in deference to his antlers. A cow can lead you through some tight jackpots. A cow's track is slimmer comparatively, but a surer sign is the way a bull tends to drag his feet more. If you come across a large track crisscrossed by a small track, you'll probably pass them by unless you want the calf. Meat hunters, even where female are legal, will prefer the fatness of a dry cow. If it's the rutting season and your moose is walking away cross country with any sign of stopping, he's a bull looking for a cow; about which more later.

Snow doesn't turn moose hunting into a sure thing, but it does give you the opportunity of dealing with imprinted facts rather than with bare guesses. When you can you follow as far downwind of the tracks as you reasonably can while still maintaining contact. Then it's mostly a matter of proceeding as inconspicuously as possible, of taking every advantage of short cuts and vantage points, and of watching all the time.

If you've never felt the breath-catching excitement of hunting moose in snow, here is a tip that can put a moose-foot ash tray beside your chair. Keep a lookout for when your moose begins to zigzag; not the haphazard excursions for food but a wide, definite pattern. This is a sign that your moose is planning to lie down. Before it does, it will probably swing back with the wind in a half circle. That way it will be in position to watch its back trail, depending on ears and nose to protect it from behind.

Keep following such booby-trapped tracks, and even if you're not heard or seen, before you reach the inside of the loop your scent will be blown warningly across the ever alert moose. Instead, look for concealment in which your quarry may be bedded; a clump of evergreen or thick bush in an otherwise parkline expanse, etc. Begin working your way slowly across wind, advancing in a cautious zigzag of your own if you have to work blind. Keep looking. Keep ready. Every next instant may be one of suddenly exploding action.

Glasses are a boon in such stalking. Until you've seen for yourself, you'll find it hard to credit that an animal as big as a horse can blend itself so inconspicuously with shadows, roots, trunks, and hummocks. Moose have a trick, too, of facing you from behind some camouflage. The last five times I've known of this happening to me, the only way I could make sure the motionless darkness was an animal was by glassing the tan-to-dark-brown gradations of the legs.

To return to tracking for a moment, one thing that can alert you to the nearness of your moose is the persistent scolding of squirrels up ahead where your quarry should be. Naturally, this is a two-edged sword, but there are three definite times when listening to such sentinels can pay off. One is when you're tracking. Another is when you're really and truly still hunting. A third is when you're set in one place, on stand maybe or in camp.

The cause of the disturbance may not be what you're hunting at the moment. But if you've a modicum of woods savvy, there's no reason for being fooled very long by a squirrel, say, who's actually chattering at you. By paying attention to the animal and bird life about you, you're an odds-on favorite to see more game than you'd even be aware of otherwise.

Speaking of wildlife, perhaps this is the time to consider that of the moose themselves. In late summer, when moose seasons are opening in the Yukon and adjoining Alaska and British Columbia, numerous bulls are fattening in high country while their antlers are hardening. Glassing from slopes and spurs, you can often see two or more in sight at the same time, near water close to the timber line. Such bulls usually are not too hard to stalk. Their meat, incidentally, is now at its best.

From approximately the full moon of September to the full moon of October, the rut is on. Now is the time that bulls are called up, an aspect of moose hunting that we'll consider shortly. A bull on the look for his lady love can be a tough article to catch.

Moose will definitely move right out of the country on you. One herd near our Peace River homesite regularly feeds from one end to the other of a mountain range forty miles long. A moose population at Tweedsmuir Park, also in British Columbia, migrates as much as seventy miles twice annually. This foot-loose characteristic is a reason why, even in the best moose country, you should allow yourself a wide margin of time.

One of the spectacles of the north woods during the rutting season is the striking, clashing duel of rival bulls, sometimes audible for miles. The winner claims from one to several cows. You'll often come upon the vanquished bulls eating dispiritedly on the edges of the herd. If what you want is meat, unless they've been wounded severely they're apt to be fatter than the boss bull. If you're fishing in moose country the following May or early June, you may see the newly born little tan calves and hear their lamblike bleats.

Moose seasons are still open in some localities when the older bulls begin shedding their antlers in December, which the younger bulls do somewhat later. When winters are mild, the antlers are often retained longer. If what you want is meat, though, now is the time for settling for a dry cow where females are legal.

In case you're more interested in heads, antler growth begins about April. Yearling bulls often have forks. The second set may bear three points per side or small palms. Moose mature in eighteen months, but ordinarily it isn't until about the fifth year that the mature type of palmate rack is developed. Maximum spreads, sometimes as wide as a basketball player is tall, are attained between the sixth and tenth years. Bulls with these rocking-chair racks are the busters every birch-horn artist is hoping someday to call up.

How does one call up a moose? An acquaintance of mine, who'd just opened a hunting camp in eastern Canada, was

The best moose hunting usually is found in wild country, and many such spots can be reached by plane. This is the Laurentians area in Quebec, Canada. (*Canadian Pacific Railway photo*)

asked that question at a sportsmen's banquet in suburban Boston. Having plenty of assurance, he cupped his hands and gave a demonstration. A few of the club members, including several successful moose hunters, told me later that night at the Sportsman's Show that it was the finest example of moose calling they'd ever heard. The point is that Sandy, who's since climbed into the upper half of the five-figure income bracket as a steel salesman, had never before in his life even tried to call up a moose.

When you realize how many sounds will attract a bull when he's in an amorous mood, you can better understand how so many guides manage to entice so many moose with so many different arias. I've even known Indians to bring them close during the lovelorn season by dragging strings of rusty tomato cans behind their horses. In other words, you've a lot of latitude in which to work.

Time never stops any stiller than when a bellowing bull is alternately crashing and pussyfooting closer, and you're wondering if one more *oooo-waughhhhh* will scare him away or lure him those final few yards. You can learn a lot about this kind of hunting by talking to old-timers, by listening to the strange, yearning sough of the cow moose in crisp fall weather, and by practicing the grunt common to moose the year round.

What one characteristic of all moose gives the hunter his biggest break? Its eating habits! A moose can stow away a ton of willow, birch, and aspen browse in well under two months. This it will happily supplement with lily roots and other aquatic starches. If things get tough, it will fill in with balsam, fir, and lodgepole pine.

With such an appetite, moose eat awhile, snooze an hour or so, and then eat some more. You're apt to find a moose eating or foraging at any time of the day. There are no waste periods. I've always been a strong believer in hunting early and late. Yet over the past twenty years, I find in checking up, I've been in on more moose kills during the kettle-boiling middle of the day than at any other time. In other words, get in the man-hours. You've only so many days, so make every minute work for you. When you're loaded for moose, every next tick of the watch may be that payoff instant.

Where across the country is the best sort of terrain to look for moose? Give the moose a chance, and it will move into a forest area that has been burned over. The young deciduous growth that springs up in such burns is its favorite browse. Tangled deadfall, furthermore, affords ideal escape routes from such enemies as wolves. While the pack is squirming under and through such jackpots, the moose is bounding over one barricade after another.

Awkward and clumsy? Colonel Townsend Whelen and I were exchanging moose experiences while writing our book *On Your Own in the Wilderness,* and the colonel told me of seeing a bull clear a fallen pine in one of the most graceful leaps he has ever witnessed. The bull didn't even leave a mark on the conifer. Yet Colonel Whelen found he could walk under that tree without stooping or touching, and he was six feet one inch tall.

In severe weather, the moose likes to take cover in evergreen stands within easy reach of hardwoods or other food. Its preference among these former is the poplar, especially live trees that have been blown down. These poplars, whose bittersweet bark the moose relishes the year round, it chaws like great ears of corn.

Here is a way you can sometimes tell in advance where to find your moose in a particular region. It doesn't work every time, and besides, some moose remain in the same limited area the year around. But there are occasions when it can give you that balance-tipping extra edge. Watch what the barometer has to tell you about the weather.

Moose fill up with food directly before really stormy weather. During heavy rain or snow, they lie up in shelter as much as possible, then feed again when the weather begins clearing. Also, moose that are ranging high in mountainous country come down before a snow storm and climb afterward. Whether you want to hunt before, during, or after such weather, a small aneroid barometer will indicate the changes well in advance. Unless one has acted on such information a few times, it will be hard to credit how vital this dope can be. One reason is that moose so impelled forget part of their natural caution.

No matter what the weather, however, with moose you've got to be ready to get into action the next split second. What is the main reason sportsmen let so many moose get away that the accompanying guides could drop easily? Marksmanship? No, the sportsman is frequently a better shot and usually better gunned. According to such a seasoned old-timer as New Brunswick outfitter Old Bill Macdonald, who was showing me some of my first moose back in the thirties, too high a percentage of otherwise topflight hunters have to wrestle their guns around too long before they start throwing lead.

Moose make large targets. Although they move away quickly, being the fastest-trotting animal in the world, they usually take off smoothly enough to give a hunter a reasonable chance to get in a shot. Some beginners always want to know, "Should I aim low the way you ought to on a deer, because a deer isn't as big as it looks?" There is only one answer to that with moose, deer, or any other game: aim exactly where you want to hit.

You'll want enough sights, enough cartridge, and enough gun. When hunting the largest deer, prehistoric or otherwise, that has ever walked this globe, a reasonable man can't afford to settle for less.

The stopping power packed into modern sporting rifles can be an awesome thing when directed against a wild animal. But there are decisive moments when the hunter needs every ounce of it. Even if personal well-being were not sometimes a factor, there's always the humane and practical desire to take game swiftly and cleanly, neither subjecting it to unnecessary suffering and possible waste, nor messing up your hunting with a lot of needless tracking and toting. This last can be particularly important when you're hunting a meat animal as big as a horse.

My experience, backed up by those of such experts as Colonel Townsend Whelen, is that the moose rifle to take is the rifle you can handle best—on up from one that will deliver a soft-point jacketed 25-caliber bullet at a muzzle velocity no slower than 2700 feet per second. If you can hit a water bucket on out to 300 yards with a good bolt-action .270 or .30/06, scope-sighted to strike at point of aim at 200 yards, that's plenty for any moose you'll ever meet.

"The neck is where I like to connect," an old sourdough told me the other fall, after I'd crossed from Whitehorse in the Yukon and was heading outside down Alaska's Inside Passage. "Mind you hit pretty nigh center, lest you miss the bone. Then you'll be eating beans a while longer, except of course you're only a mite low and slice the juggler."

That's pretty much the story on the much touted neck shot. The brain shot is even more limited. It's a fact that nothing equals it for sheer drama, but . . . Well, maybe you've also split open a few moose heads to get at this grayish mass of nerve tissue. It's true that its delicate flavor goes well with eggs, which can be scrambled in the same pan after the highly nutritious brains have been rolled in seasoned bread crumbs, dipped in beaten egg, recrumbed, and then fried golden brown. But there is more volume to a large grapefruit.

If you want to take the brain shot, perhaps as a finisher on a moose whose head you won't be keeping as a trophy, air an imaginary bull's-eye: (1) From the side, midway along a line connecting the eye and ear cavities; (2) From the front, between and a trifle above the eyes. Just hitting the moose's huge head even with a 500-grain .458 or better won't do the job, although such shooting does tear away jaws and cause other wounds that spell slow death and wasted game.

The lung shot is deadly. The heart shot is seldom quicker. When the lower portions of this organ are hit, it is not always so sudden. The only reason why the so-called "heart shot" isn't less effective is that many sportsmen do not realize how low in a moose the heart actually lies. Therefore, a lot of well, if mistakenly, aimed bullets strike high and disrupt the great arteries above the heart. Here they both rapidly flood the vital chest area and stop the life-maintaining flow of blood to the brain.

The killing shot that affords the most margin for error? One aimed to enter the center of the chest cavity.

The best combined stopper and killer? That's the immobilizing, paralyzing, deadly shot into or between the shoulders, in line with the forelegs one third of the way down the body. A reasonably near miss with any well-penetrating bullet—on up from the previously suggested minimum—will, out to about 200 yards in the case of the minimum, guarantee you ample time for a finisher.

If, like a few million other sportsmen you get a thrill out of the ultimate moment when you knock over a deer, then you haven't really lived until you look down the sights at a half ton or more of moose.

A couple of final tips? If you're going moose hunting, get in shape first. This is particularly important if you are going in by horse. But no matter how you travel, take a little more time at this stage and really get back into wild country where, as they say, the hand of man has never set foot. There, if you want a moose badly enough to work for it, the odds are that you'll connect and collect big. Tough? Well, if it is, it'll be worth it.

Chapter Seventeen

BLACK-BEAR WAYS

by FRANK C. HIBBEN

FRANK C. HIBBEN is a professor of anthropology and Director of the Museum at the University of New Mexico and is widely known as a big-game hunter and author. He started hunting at the age of twelve and shot his first grizzly bear at the age of fifteen. Since that time he has bagged a large variety of animals all over the world. He has hunted or collected animals for a museum in most of the United States, Alaska, Canada, Mexico, Central America, Europe, the Near East, Asia, and Africa. These adventures have resulted in numerous articles and stories he has written for the leading general and outdoor magazines. His books include *Hunting American Lions, Hunting American Bears,* and the recent *Hunting in Africa.*

THE American black bear is one of our most interesting and least known game animals. Many American hunters have never seen a black bear outside of a national park, and this is no accident. The bruin, like the red fox, has learned to get along with civilization and modern man mainly by avoiding them. It probably takes more knowledge, more skill, and more endurance to bag a bear than any other kind of American big game.

Professional predator men, after a stock-killing or nuisance bear, use traps. Under certain circumstances, black bears are easy to trap. However, trapping is not considered "fair chase" and therefore is to be ignored as a hunting method. The same is true of the more odious use of poison for killing black bears. The infamous poison, 1080, injected into a chunk of meat, is death on black bears, especially when they come out of hibernation in the spring. Anything which has nibbled 1080 bait and died and is subsequently eaten by a bear will also kill that bear. In places where 1080 has been used carelessly, the black-bear population has been virtually wiped out.

Frank C. Hibben.

For legitimate hunters not interested in trapping or Borgia methods of bagging a bruin, there are three ways of bear hunting. These are still hunting, tracking, and the use of dogs. Although these three bear-hunting methods vary in different parts of America, as do the laws which govern them, all three require an intimate knowledge of bear habits on the part of the hunter.

Still hunting is legal everywhere that black bears are found and is the universal method employed by most hunters during the bear season. However, many a veteran deer hunter who fancies himself a good woodsman and naturalist has never glimpsed a bear.

In areas where black bears are harried by humans, the bruin has become almost entirely nocturnal. However, even with his night habits, his instinct and his pattern of life will betray him to the hunter who knows that pattern.

Bears, like human beings, are omnivorous. They will eat anything. The would-be hunter first must discover if there are any bears in his hunting territory and then find out what the bears are eating at that particular time of year. In any given piece of hunting terrain, the bear's diet will differ according to climatic factors (i.e. "a good berry year") and may differ considerably from year to year. A bear hunter starting out on a five-day hunt will do well to spend four days finding out what the bears are eating.

In certain areas, such as Alaska, the diet of the bear is fairly obvious and is determined by natural happenings which are routine. When the salmon are running in the streams, the black bears will be catching fish, especially at certain tidal pools and below waterfalls where the salmon congregate. At one such place in Alaska, which was shown to me by an Alaskan hunter who shot black bears to sell their hides, I saw and photographed forty-four black bears in a single morning at one salmon pool. Shooting a bruin at such a place would be an anticlimax.

Also in northern regions, black bears habitually feed on blueberries when they are ripe. Finding a berry patch across a mountain canyon and locating the jet-black form of a feeding bear is fairly easy in that kind of country.

But in Pennsylvania, New York, the southern states, or the

Far West, the still hunting of black bear is a difficult and knowledgeable business. As the hunting season usually comes in the fall, the autumn feeding habits of the black bear concern us most. At this time, bears are feeding continually to lay up fat for hibernation. Hibernation is a matter of fat and body condition and not necessarily of weather. A fat bear in a year of plentiful food will hibernate early. In a lean year, a thin bear may still be tramping the snow-covered mountains in search of food in November or December. In a very bad season black bears may invade a town for garbage or descend into valley farmlands to lay on enough fat so as to sleep the remainder of the winter. The urge to eat may carry the feeding bruin into the daylight hours so that the hunter can have a look at him. In places, black bears may still be eating grass and roots in the fall, especially if no other food is available. The vegetable-feeding bear may vary his diet by raiding a farmer's potato field; or an apple orchard may be the attraction. Far more likely, the fall feeding black bear will locate a patch of acorns, beechnuts, piñon nuts, wild rose hips, chokecherries, or some other favorite food, even though the spot may be miles from his normal terrain. In the western states black bears travel far out of the mountains to feed on piñon nuts in the foothills. If the piñon crop is scanty and there are few acorns, juniper berries, in spite of their bitter taste, are a staple, or even the fruit of the prickly pear cactus.

Whatever the food of the moment might be in any particular area, the black bear is a creature of habit, and this is where the hunter comes in. If a bear has located a little valley where the acorn crop is heavy, the bear will visit the area nightly until the acorns are gone. Chances are, several other bears will be there too. A potential bear hunter, if he can locate such a spot, is three fourths of the way to having a nice rug on the wall of his trophy room.

At the beginning of a bear hunt, up-to-date information is the most valuable weapon a hunter can have. The presence of bears and their feeding is determined by the droppings. A hunter casing through a stretch of territory can determine by the droppings and the tracks the number of bears feeding in an

Black bears are notoriously shy and elusive animals and rarely come out in the open like this female and her cubs. Semi-tame black bears in parks or around garbage dumps, however, often tolerate people. (*Canadian Government Travel Bureau photo*)

area and what they are eating. Even if the tracking is over impossible terrain, an occasional imprint will show the direction of the berry patch or mast plot which the bruins are using. Once the hunter gets into the area, he will have no difficulty in recognizing the spot. Black bears are not subtle in their feeding. They tear the limbs off trees, often riding the branches down with the weight of their bodies so as to strip the fruit from the tips. An apple orchard where three or four blacks have been feeding looks like the aftermath of a tornado and hailstorm combined. Sow bears with cubs are especially destructive, breaking down whole trees with their powerful paws so that the cubs can feed on the fruit.

Another help to the hunter is that black bears water every day and during heavy feeding twice a day. They usually water at the same place, especially after a bellyful of dry acorns or vegetable food. In the western states where water is scarce, it is often possible to locate a water hole or a stock tank which a feeding bear visits every twelve hours or so.

When the bear hunter has located a feeding spot or a water hole which the bruins have used within the last twelve hours, his next concern in a stakeout. My own preference is for a tree, although I admit this is uncomfortable after a few hours. From a tree, a hunter can see better, and an approaching bear has less chance of scenting danger. A stakeout on the ground is difficult in an oak grove or berry patch, since the bear may well approach and begin feeding without the hunter's getting a shot. The main thing to remember is that black bears have an extraordinary acute sense of smell and hearing. The hunter should be in position before the bear comes to feed. A convenient rimrock, a perch on a fallen tree or stump, or a small open glade may be the setup for a hunter to get a shot as the bear comes in. The main thing to watch is the direction of the wind. Usually if the bear has fed at the spot before, he will come in from the same direction as before and will not be too careful. But the bear will always put his nose into the wind and wrinkle his snout before he begins to feed.

In hunted areas, black bears normally feed at night and curl up in some cozy, deep timber hideout during the day. However, as the urge to hibernate is strong upon them, they will begin to feed about four o'clock in the afternoon and will continue to feed into the morning daylight hours. In the early morning the hunter has the disadvantage of having to approach the feeding spot. Unless there is a wind to cover the noise of his approach, a wary bruin will hear the shuffling of human feet and slip silently away. The evening time is best, as the hunter can get in position early in the afternoon. When the bear climbs a tree for his first mouthful, or stands on his hind legs to sniff the wind, the hunter will have his chance, and he should be ready.

One admonition to the bear hunter. It does not take a big gun to kill a black bear, but the shot must be placed with great care. A bear should be shot through the shoulders or through the neck. A bear shot behind the shoulders, even through the lungs, can run for a mile and probably will do so.

Although the number of black-bear attacks on human beings is relatively small, the black bear is a very powerful animal and can kill a man with one blow of his paw or crunch of his jaws. Don't let a black bear get close to you and don't walk up to a wounded bear even if you think he is finished. Shoot him through the shoulders and keep shooting until you are sure he is dead.

A number of bear hunters have had remarkable success tracking bears, although the conditions have to be just right for this method. Snow, of course, is ideal. Some hunters have successfully tracked bears in mud. Often the first snow will catch a bear not yet fat enough for hibernation, especially in a year when acorns and berries are scarce. Bears too thin to sleep travel widely in search of food and often will raid farms or even garbage cans to fill out their bellies. In a tracking snow, the hunter can follow them and usually catch up to the quarry as the bear stops to dig out mice, roots, or eat frost-shriveled grass. On a bear track, the main thing is silence. If the snow crunches or your boots squeak, your chances of seeing a bear are slim.

For really serious bear hunting, dogs are the answer. Trailing dogs are illegal in some states and may not be used under other circumstances as, for example, when the deer season is in progress. The use of hounds is not, as some hunters would claim, un-

A black bear leaves a double row of tracks which indicate the direction
of travel and size of the animal.

sportsmanlike or too easy. Quite the contrary. A bear chase
with trained dogs requires as much know-how as any other
method and a lot more endurance.

Bear dogs are usually trained hounds of mixed breeds. A good
bear dog can be a bloodhound, foxhound, blue tick, Walker,
or a combination of these. Even airedales are sometimes used. A
successful bear hound must have the nose of a French connois-
seur, the speed of a Kentucky Derby winner, and the ferocity
of a jaguar. A running bear can go about fifteen miles an hour
and can keep it up for a long time. A thin bear can run seem-
ingly forever. A fat bear will usually bolt a short distance and
then turn and fight. If the dogs do not know their business, a
bayed bear can tear up a whole dog pack in less time than it
takes to tell about it.

The training of a good pack of bear dogs is, then, an exacting
business which may take years. The dogs must be broken from
the running of deer, baying at turtles, snapping at porcupines,

killing chickens, chasing pigs, or other things that bear dogs are not supposed to do. The dog trainer must point out to the dog that he is supposed to chase bear and only bear and then hold the quarry until the hunter can come up and make his shot. A good bear hound must be as hardheaded as a Roman soldier to stick to his job. The bear-dog owner must be even more determined. A great many hounds of good breeding never make the grade. A really good bear dog may be worth as much as a thousand dollars by the time he is fully trained.

Fortunately, unlike grizzlies, black bears can climb trees and usually do when pursued by dogs. A heavy bear hampered by winter fat may have so much difficulty getting up a tree that he will elect to fight it out on the ground. A very thin bear, or one which has escaped from inept dogs on a previous occasion, may elect to run and keep running. The job of the dogs is to get to the bear, bay him or tree him, and keep him there until the hunter can catch up. Many a good trailing hound is poor at a tree. One of the best bear dogs I ever saw would tree a bear and then turn around and come back to the hunter with his tongue lolling and his tail wagging as though the job were done. A good tree dog is one which will get the bear up a tree and then sit under it barking his head off, so that the hunter can find the spot. Usually when a bear has climbed a tree to escape the tormenting hounds, old bruin will rest awhile. Then, when his panting has stopped, he will climb down the tree, back foremost, and run again. A good tree dog, or better yet, a pack of them, when old bruin backs down that tree, must chew on the bear so convincingly that the quarry climbs back up again. This takes some doing with a big and determined bear.

Professional bear hunters, or those who make a business of running bear with hounds, usually have one or two "jump dogs" in the pack. These dogs are curs of mixed breed, airedales, part bulldogs, or anything canine that has a lot of speed, ferocity, and noise. Hounds will trail the bears by using their noses. A jump dog uses his eyes and his mouth. Once the game is jumped and leaves cover, the fierce jump dog immediately gets to the bear and begins to harass him. He does this by slashing at the bruin's hindquarters and flanks. The dogs quickly learn to work

Unlike grizzlies, black bears are good tree climbers. The most effective way of hunting them in the West is to chase them with dogs until they are treed. This can be done only in states where hunting with dogs is legal.

with each other. As the bear turns to snap or bite at one, the others will rush in from the opposite side to nip at the quarry. A fighting jump dog either learns very quickly or he is dead.

In our bear pack of some years ago, we had an airedale named Poncho. Poncho would rush up to a running bear, jump on his back, and ride the bruin like a jockey. With Poncho biting at the bear's neck and two or three other dogs around his flank, that bear usually took to a tree and quickly. On one occasion, a very large chocolate-colored bear climbed a tree with Poncho clinging to his hump with locked teeth. Once up in the pine tree, the bear reached over his back, pulled Poncho loose, and bit the dog through the head. Fortunately, the bear's teeth skidded on Poncho's skull. The powerful jaws of the bear scalped Poncho but did not kill him. Next year, when the awful wound had healed, Poncho was back riding bears again.

With a good hound pack and one or two jump dogs, the bear hunter usually cuts through bear country between the feeding areas and water. If the feed areas are known, there are apt to be too many tracks where two or three bears have been circling and climbing oak trees during a night's feeding. The ideal situation is to catch a bear early in the morning with his belly heavy with feed and on his way to water. Unfortunately, the hunter seldom gets exactly what he would like and must be ready for anything.

Hounds will follow a fresh bear track just as enthusiastically backward as they will in the right direction. They don't look— they smell. A bear hound can smell the scent from a fresh track without even putting his nose to the ground. A "stinking old bruin" will leave so much scent that a hound can smell the trail several yards away. If there is a cross wind, the dogs will run the bear to the side of the actual track and downwind.

A keen-eyed hunter may find the track first, keeping his dogs well behind him. This will allow the hunter to see the direction of the track and the size. It may be a yearling bear, not good game, or, worse yet, a female with cubs. Sows with cubs are illegal prey in most places and, in any event, not a sporting quarry for a true bear hunter.

Usually hounds ranging in the brush are the first ones to pick up the track. There is nothing that a bear dog likes to do so well as bark on a bear track. In a hound pack, every dog knows his fellows better than their owner. If a "true" hound barks, the other dogs know that the bark means bear, and they are off in the matter of seconds. If the hunter is a little behind or a mite slow, his whole dog pack may be gone after the wrong bear or in the wrong direction before he ever gets started.

Usually, for hound hunting, the bear hunter should be mounted and on a fast horse. Without a good mountain horse, the bear and hounds will be out of hearing in a few minutes, and the hunter will be out of the chase. The foot hunter with dogs must be a hardy type—I might even say foolhardy. Bears can go miles in minutes. So can dogs. When harassed by hounds, the bear will instinctively take to the roughest country or the thickest timber to shake off his pursuers. An old bear-hunter friend of mine once remarked, "It all looks level to a bear."

Once the dogs are on the right end of the right track, the hunter must look to himself to keep in the chase. A horse that has been used in several bear hunts usually is infected with the enthusiasm of the barking dogs and heads toward the sound. Low limbs, loose rocks, badger holes, dead tree stubs in the midst of concealing brush, and a thousand other hazards will loom up before the galloping bear hunter without the chance to avoid them. Even veteran bear hunters will run their horses over country where they would not lead a mount if they stopped to think about it. They simply don't stop to think. "It's crazy dangerous, but it's the most exciting hunting I've ever done," remarked one novice after he had ridden to his first bear with our dog pack. The excitement of the bear chase itself is augmented by hearing the hounds at their work. At the end is the bear in a tree or bayed on the ground and the expectation of closing in on a very dangerous adversary.

Even with good hounds on a good track, the outcome is uncertain until the last shot is fired. The dogs can cross from a fresh track to an old one. The bear may double and the dogs end up running the track the wrong way. Actually a black bear can get away from any dog if he learns his own strength. If he runs and fights, even veteran hounds will have to give up after several hours. The hunter on the track of a running bear will find only a pack of weary dogs at the end of a long day's hunt.

If you hunt with hounds, a few admonitions are necessary. When the bear is treed, don't ride up to the dogs whooping and yelling like a Comanche. The bear, seeing a hunter gallop up, will invariably shinny down the tree and be off. If the dogs are tired, they may never catch him again. The hunter should slip up quietly, talking in whispers to his companions, until he is actually under the bear tree.

To a dog there is no such thing as a poor shot. When the gun goes off, the bear is dead as far as the hounds are concerned. They have run a long way and done a lot of barking for a chance to chaw on that carcass, and they're not going to miss it. Without a second's hesitation and in one bawling, milling mass, every dog in the pack will be on the bear the moment he hits ground, dead or alive. A wounded bear can kill dogs faster than the dogs can close in. A fighting bear with dogs all over him is a difficult mark for a careless hunter. If the hunter wades in to finish his work at close range, he probably will be bitten by the bear or the dogs or both before it is finished. A careful shot through the shoulders is best, so that the powerful front paws of the bear are immobilized before he tumbles down out of the tree. If the bear is looking down at the rifleman, the shot up through the neck is a good one and immediately fatal.

By any method of hunting, the successful black-bear hunter can count himself in the same class with Daniel Boone.

218   F. Phillips Williamson.

Chapter Eighteen

GRIZZLY AND BROWN BEARS

by F. PHILLIPS WILLIAMSON

F. PHILLIPS WILLIAMSON is a realtor, appraiser, and counselor who lives on Maryland's eastern shore at Cambridge. That is, you'll find him there if he isn't somewhere in the great outdoors hunting. You name the game animal or game bird and Phil Williamson has probably shot it. He has taken record-book walrus, brown bear, black bear, jaguar, and a number of African species. He has hunted in most of the United States, Canada, Alaska, and has now taken twenty-three of the twenty-five legal species of North American big game. He has also hunted in Europe, Central America, and made two major safaris to Africa. His library on shooting and ballistics is considered one of the three largest in the Unites States.

EVERY big-game hunter seems to ask the question—where is the best place to go for an umpteen-foot bear or a sheep with three curls and a button. Certain of our species of North American big game are found in very limited areas, especially brown bears and grizzly bears.

The Williamson "almost sure-fire method" of getting a grizzly is quite simple—get your gear together and take off, not after grizzly but sheep! If you get your sheep the first day out, then spend every hour trying to photograph more sheep (with your rifle along, of course!). If you get tired of this or run out of film, climb a mountain every morning at first light and be there when the sun comes up; then be on a different mountain when the sun goes down. After a two- to three-week hunt, the chances are 60–40 that you'll get a shot at a grizzly.

I hasten to point out that the above method's odds prevail only in Alaska, British Columbia, and the Yukon. There are grizzlies in Alberta, Montana, and Wyoming but few in number. Every once in a while rumors run hot and heavy that a grizzly is spotted in the Middle Fork country of Idaho, but a closed season prevails and the verification is yet to be made. The grizzly hunts in Wyoming can be successful—sure, but I'd put the odds at 96 to 4 in favor of the bear. If you insist on a hunt in Wyoming, the best hunt is a spring hunt.

However, the first part of the spring hunt has to be started in late fall or early winter. Retain (that is pay out cash) your outfitter to walk in an old horse or mule just before the snow gets too deep and shoot same for bait. If baiting is not legal, then elk, deer, or cow winter kill must be found. The choice of the spot is quite limited—it has to be near the line of Yellowstone Park—I'd suggest the head of the Yellowstone River. Then, as soon as the mountain passes are passable, be there! If Wyoming permits an open season on grizzly by then, you have one chance in twenty-five of getting a shot at a grizzly. The bait must be checked every day from downwind at long range (a spotting scope pays off). If lady luck smiles at you and the sun works the bait over, something will be having a spring feed. Now to determine what. A location downwind of the bait varies with the time of day. Usually you can depend on the wind blowing down the canyon in the morning and up the canyon in the afternoon. Naturally, the time for the bear to appear is at first light or at dusk. The observation point should be within 200 yards of the bait, and the way to this spot can be marked with toilet paper for travel in the dark. Horses should be left no less than three quarters of a mile away with a wrangler (don't forget, bear are hungry in the spring). Odds are that the diner at the bait will be a black bear or coyote. If you're lucky and a grizzly appears just make sure it's not a sow with cubs before you pop the primer!

Grizzly in Montana or Alberta are nearly as scarce, so let's take a good look at the north country. Alaska, Yukon, or British Columbia grizzly hunting is much the same—hunt stone or Dall's sheep and your chances are good to get a grizzly. You'll look over the finest game country in North America, reduce your waistline, and, at the same time, enjoy food that sold for a higher price than beef in the old gold-rush camps—sheep meat. If you are not the first party your outfitter brought into the area that fall, ask him where he saw the most wild berries, then do your sheep-grizzly hunting in that area. Watch the high slopes, the berry patches, old moose or caribou kills, and, if you are the last party, watch the rock slides—grizzlies often dig for marmots, a last snack before the long winter sleep.

When you spot your grizzly, take off on a stalk right away! These bears move and will take off at the slightest sour man scent or sound. While a bear's eyesight is not supposed to be keen, don't take chances. You're after one of the rarest big-game species in North America. Travel low, slow, out of sight, soft, and upwind. Try to keep a ridge or some obstruction between you and the spot where you last saw the bear. Make sure of the wind—if you're unlucky enough to spot the bear in the middle of the day when the wind tends to eddy, you're in for trouble. I've tried leaves, dust, and pipe smoke, but the best way I've found to determine wind direction is wood ashes. A small leather pouch with a fold-over top filled with fine dry wood ashes is the best wind-direction indicator. Sift a few often—remember, one whiff of man scent and *Ursus horribilis* is long gone.

If possible, make the stalk so that you're either opposite or above the bear for the shot. Best shot for a stopper is a high shoulder shot, with one exception: if the bear appears directly up the mountain above you, I'm a firm believer in a brain shot regardless of the fact that the skull will be ruined for Boone and Crockett measurement. As soon as the bear is shot, he will roll —directly toward you—keep pumping lead! I've had such a shot on grizzly that we spotted feeding on berries near the head of a draw; the only stalk possible was up the draw, and the shot had to be made with the bear directly above or he would have topped out and been gone. That bear rolled directly toward my position. I shot for the brain first but could not be sure whether the bear was stunned or dead, so, as he was rolling, I made two more shots into the lung-heart-shoulder section. Then I jumped aside. After the bear was skinned out, I found that the 130-gr. .270 Silvertip first shot was all that was necessary— the other two were not needed—the bear was dead at the first shot. We rolled the skin down the mountain, took a handkerchief soaked with the blood of the bear and tied it over the nose of the guide's horse, loaded on the bearskin, and headed back to camp. The shot was made at 4 P.M., and we got back to camp at 9:30. Those horses knew the way better than we did in the dark.

You will note that I have not suggested spring hunts for grizzlies in the north country. As grizzlies come out of hibernation in early May, their fur certainly is heavy and prime. But they tend to travel more after the first week of leaving their den, and besides, sheep season is closed.

Firepower for grizzly begins in my Bible with a .270 and runs through the .30/06, .300 Weatherby Magnum, .300 Winchester Magnum back to the Remington 7X Magnum using the 175 gr. Core-lokt bullet. I've used them all on bear but this 7X Remington Magnum is something to behold. I have shot two bear (not through the brain either) with mine in the two years since it has been on the market. One went 10 yards, the other 10 feet, and neither required a second shot! Scope, of course, is either a 4X or one of the varipower like the 3X–9X Redfield or the B&L.

Special clothing for grizzly hunting includes a good pair of leather shoes that lace well and are *broken in,* and soles should be of the heavy rubber lug type. A down jacket, wool pants, and some lightweight rain gear that will fold and fit in the side pocket of the down jacket will complete the outfit. An extra belt is handy—when you are climbing, take the jacket off, fold it over, run your belt through the fold, and put it to your back. When you top out, the jacket provides a good chill preventer. Obtain a drop-point skinning knife (like Randall's Alaskan) and an ax stone. Last but not least, be sure to take and *use* a good pair of field glasses. Get a pair of "night" glasses—you'll do the most of the looking early and late. The Hensoldt roof-prism 8×56 are large, but their light-gathering qualities are something to behold.

Now we come to that other giant bear—the brown bear—which is the biggest flesh-eating land animal in the world today. Brown bear are in four areas that require different methods of hunting. These are the Alaska Peninsula, Kodiak Island, the area around Yakutat and Russell Fiord to Dry Bay and the Baranof and Admiralty Island area of Southeast Alaska.

On the Alaska Peninsula, when the section around Port Heiden and Port Mollar was open, the only method was to fly in via Super Cub equipped with the doughnut low-pressure large tires or the tandem gear. On one trip we had the planes flown out from Anchorage and we got them at King Salmon. We would fly up the many unnamed rivers emptying into the Bering Sea until we reached the divide of the watershed between the Bering Sea and the Pacific Ocean. If a plot of tundra some 400 feet long could be found, we'd land, set up camp, and hunt on foot out of that area. This was in the spring. Snowbanks and slopes were glassed (between storms), and many brownies were often seen each day in this springtime hunting. I've never been there in the fall, but the bear would be down near the Bering Sea, feeding on salmon spawning in the stream. Camp still would have to be made at least up in the alders in order to have a source for firewood. Because weight was so important, we only used one pair of boots for each two hunters—when a stream had to be waded the boots were tossed back to the other side! I believe there are more record-book bear on the Peninsula than anywhere else in Alaska.

Special gear for this area includes a gasoline stove for cooking, a small Yukon-type stove for heat, and a tent that you can guy and hold down in an 80 m.p.h. wind. One spinning rod and reel and a half-dozen red-and-white "Dardevles" will keep a camp in fresh Dolly Varden trout. Observe while you are in this area the caribou—these are the Grant variety and are nearly white in May.

The best time on the Peninsula seems to be the first three weeks in May. The big, old boar should be out first, and their coats are prime. If you spot a bear curled up asleep in a snow bank, you can bet it will be a boar with an unrubbed coat. In the fall the bear will be feeding all along the salmon streams. The stalk here is upwind and upstream, if possible, with a lot of looking and slow movement.

The Kodiak Island hunt generally is equally successful in the spring and fall. The method of hunting is from a base camp at

Alaskan brown bears will be found along the streams in the fall, feeding on salmon.

a lodge or quarters of a comfortable boat. This type has the advantage of a warm, dry bed and good food every night (well, almost), and a skiff can be used on mild days to cover the coast line. You look for fresh bear tracks on the snow-sided mountains in the spring or bear feeding along the streams in the fall. Once the bear is spotted, the stalk begins at once. If the alders are thick, you may not see the bear until you literally bump into him or he hears you and stands up to see what another animal is doing in his territory. Crawling along a bear trail through alders is rough on somebody my size, but trying to cut straight through alders is very difficult. Alders seem to come out of the ground, grow one to three feet along the ground, then continue their vertical growth.

I shot a record-book brownie one day on the Peninsula at seventy-five yards in heavy alders. I had spotted the bear in a snowbank from a mountain lookout. I'll bet it took me ten minutes at least to fight my way through these alders before I reached the bear. Matter of fact, the only way I ever got a shot was after getting my marks lined up where I thought the bear was; then I shouted, and with that the bear stood up. One shot with the Winchester Model 70, .375 H&H (300-gr. Silvertip) did the trick with a heart and spine shot as he stood up on his hind legs, facing me. A lucky break for me, too, since the pin holding the ejector sheared off after working the bolt on this shot!

In the Icy Bay, Russell Fiord, Yakutat, and Dry Bay section of Alaska, the spring hunt usually means living out of a boat or cabin and watching the beaches, slides, and slopes. In the Yakutat section, it is possible to get black bear (and, if your totem is right, glacier bear) and brownies in the same area. In the fall the brownies do not always come to the salmon streams when the fish are running. Quite often when there is a big berry crop, the bear will feed in the high country until the berries are nearly gone and then come down for the last of the salmon run. However, if the berry crop is small, you can bet the bear will be on the streams by September 1. In this area a fall hunt has to be planned with the best possible forecast for the berry crop. I remember in 1957 planning a big hunt in the Yakutat area for brown bear. We were there three weeks, and I never got a chance to look through the scope at a bear. I found out where the bear were, all right, after I chartered a Seabee and flew up in the high country. There were berries everywhere and bears too. Our outfit was too big to move, and the bear had just started to come out on the high reaches of the streams when we left.

The next fall I stopped in Juneau en route to British Columbia; the Fish and Wildlife people told me bear were on the beaches, and that was the last of August! It all goes to show you that you must be flexible. We had some heavy gear and had lined up for a "soft" hunt. We flew in rubber life rafts and gear to Situk Lake, fished awhile, scouted, then floated the Situk River to the old cannery rail line. The fall before, one of our group had done this and come out with some wonderful brown-bear movies. We would have had to have lightweight alpine tents and bags to get high enough to hunt these bear. In that country there often is

300 inches of snow plus 150 inches of rain. We had rain every day for two weeks at one period.

Special gear for this rain country must include a two-piece waterproof (not water-resistant) rain suit. I'd also suggest rubber kitchen gloves, boots, and a waterproof plastic rifle bag. All clothes should be inside double plastic freezer bags. One good trick is a pair of yellow glasses and a cowboy hat over the rain-suit parka hood. Sure it will get wet, but it will hold the parka of the rain suit in place so you can turn your head without your vision being blocked, and water will be shed away from your face and neck. For your boots, try a special pair of suspenders where the bootstraps will snap into them directly under your arms and not be dragging at your belt all day.

Get used to shooting a scoped rifle in the rain—you'll need practice. Coat the rifle bedding with a grease like that used in water pumps, and put it together and target—it will help to keep moisture out. And, finally, wear all-*wool* clothes. Soaking wet, they will keep you warm where wet cotton would freeze you. You'll also need some kind of super-duper fire starter when light wood is scarce.

The hunting in southeastern Alaska is usually done using a large boat like Petersburg veteran guide Ralph Young's 46-foot *Umatilla*. Here four hunters sleep forward in a heated cabin with head, while Ralph and his assistants sleep aft. A good galley, Deepfreeze, and Ralph's wife, Jo, assure the party of good food. The boat can stand a lot of heavy weather often found in the Admiralty and Baranof Island section. Hunting here is both spring and fall with the bear in rugged terrain and hard to find in late spring but concentrated along the salmon streams in the fall. Clothing here is about the same, except that generally it has to be warmer than that used in the Yakutat area.

For all brown-bear areas the rifles best regarded are the .375 H&H Magnum, .300 Weatherby Magnum, .30/06 (220-gr. bullet), the .338 Alaskan with the .375 H&H the most favored. This is not without good reason. Tuned up, the .375 H&H will really shoot a tight group. Its knockdown power leaves nothing to be desired in Alaska, and the bullet can penetrate a mass of alders if it has to in order to get the job done. Sights should not be over 2½X to 3X for brown bear, and I like a rifle where the scope can be quickly detached and iron sights, like the Griffen and Howe double lever, used for follow-up of wounded game.

Take a box of ammo, the same skinning knife and field glasses used for grizzly, and a lot of reading literature. Pick out a good spot or stream, cover a quarter of the ground that you would ordinarily in twice the time. Stop, look, and look some more. Watch your wind—that bear you just spooked would be number one in the record book!

228   Carlos Vinson.

Chapter Nineteen

WHEN YOU TACKLE WILD BOARS

by CARLOS VINSON

CARLOS VINSON was born in the hills of central Tennessee where he spent his boyhood hunting, fishing, and trapping. Later he traveled over a good share of the United States and sections of Canada and came back home and settled in the little country town of McMinnville, Tennessee, not far from where he lived as a youth. Soon after he settled down and married he started writing about his outdoor experiences and has been at it ever since. His articles and stories have appeared in outdoor magazines, gun magazines, and men's, adventure, and general periodicals. He also writes a weekly hunting and fishing column for a newspaper.

THE first wild boar I ever shot at was coming straight toward me with the hair on his back bristling and his tusks snapping. The hair on my head was standing up almost as straight as the bristling hair on the boar's back.

When the wicked-looking critter was forty feet from me I pulled the trigger on my .30/30 carbine. The soft-nosed bullet plowed up loose dirt between the boar's front feet. He turned and took off down the mountainside in high gear. The hair started easing back down on my head. I was too excited to get off another shot. Five mixed-breed hounds roared through, hot on the trail of the exotic tusker.

There was a kangaroo-court session in camp that night. I got the tail of a nine-dollar flannel shirt amputated. Three other members of the party got the same treatment. Some had been more lucky. Three boars were bagged that day by a party of thirty hunters. We were hunting in the wild and rugged mountains of western North Carolina.

Matter of fact, we were hunting near the top of Hooper Bald Mountain near where the original 14 Prussian wild boars were released back in 1912. As far as is known, all the exotic wild boars in the United States today came from this original shipment of 14 which were released on a fenced portion of a private preserve and later escaped. The herd had increased to about 50 by the time they escaped. They thrived fairly well in the rugged mountains of western North Carolina and eastern Tennessee, and today there are probably around 3000 of them roaming the area. The Prussian wild boar is on the game list in both these southern states.

I have been on quite a few wild-boar hunts since I missed the one coming straight at me. If the critter had been wounded or cornered I would have lost my shirt tail before the kangaroo court session in camp that night. Might have lost some skin and blood also. Under certain conditions these animals can be very dangerous. As long as they are not wounded and running ahead of hounds they are not apt to charge a hunter. But this I did not know when I missed the one coming at me.

The usual system for hunting the wild boar in this country is to place hunters on stands near known runs and crossings; then the guide and a couple of helpers head for the previously located boar feeding grounds with five or six well-trained boar dogs. The usual pack consists of three or four hounds, ordinarily of mixed breeding, and a couple of airedales that more or less specialize in fighting the tuskers.

A boar may run for hours ahead of a pack of hounds, or he may back up against a ledge to fight it out with the baying pack after running for thirty minutes or so. They are as unpredictable as the wind. Hunters in a boar party have to be constantly on the alert. The noise of a chase may run tuskers not being chased out by any one of the standers. If the dogs chase a boar by a stander the shooting will be at a rapidly moving target in most cases.

Standers must also listen carefully for a sudden change in the tone of the chase. Chase music, once the boar is actually jumped, is usually rhythmic and unbroken, but once the boar stops and the hounds start baying and fighting the tone changes entirely. Whining yelps and uneven, excited bawls tell the hunters that the boar is at bay. Chances for a kill here are good. Standers nearest to the spot where the boar comes to bay should advance toward the spot with caution, and make ready for instant action. A boar at bay will charge hunters and dogs with equal vengeance. A charge usually means that the boar will momentarily break free of the circle of baying dogs. If the dogs are well trained and experienced, the charge will probably be unsuccessful and give one of the hunters a chance to get in a quick killing shot without fear of hitting a dog. It is when the boar charges and breaks through the circle of baying dogs that the hunter wants to shoot. The boar will not have had time to gain much speed, and if the hunter can keep his nerves calm enough this type of shot will be easy.

A boar running full speed ahead, usually in heavy undergrowth, makes a tough target—much tougher than a bayed boar. Boars flushed out of hiding places by the noise of a chase will usually also be moving much slower than those running ahead of hounds.

The Prussian wild boars in this country are very much rugged territory animals. They seem to prefer rough and rocky country high up in the mountains where there are plenty of laurels and other undergrowth. They feed on acorns, beech mast, roots, herbs, snails, salamanders, wild fruits, and on occasion even snakes and turtles. There's nothing one of the critters enjoys better than to dine on a rattlesnake.

Only poor mast years will drive these animals down into the valleys. The more successful boar hunters first determine what the feeding conditions are and then proceed to find out where the boars are feeding just before their hunt is to take place. The pre-hunt scouting, of course, is done without dogs, so that the tuskers will not be unduly disturbed and scattered before the hunt.

Some wild-boar hunting preserves are now operating in the mountains and roughs of Tennessee and Arkansas. By the time this sees print other states may very well have similar preserves. These preserves are actually commercial hunting projects, but there is very little difference between the quality of the hunting and that already described. The boars on the private preserves are identically the same animals as those found in western North Carolina and eastern Tennessee.

I recently had the pleasure of hunting on one of these preserves. There were twelve of us in the party, and we hunted over close to 4000 acres of wild mountain territory, which was owned by the preserve. This 4000 acres was under fence through which the animals could not escape—a far better and more modern fencing job than the fenced area from which the original fourteen boars and their offspring escaped.

We did not use dogs on this hunt because the guides told us that our chances of making quick kills would be "considerably better without dogs."

The mast (especially acorn) crop was lush in the eastern Tennessee mountains that fall (this preserve is in Blount County, Tennessee), and the guides knew just where a dozen or more of the tuskers were feeding regularly.

Hunters were placed on stands at various points around the feeding area near deer and other wild-animal runs leading away from the feeding nook. My stand was about sixty yards above a deer run on a steep mountainside. Three other hunters were on stands above the same run.

We heard the guide and his helpers as they started beating the brush with sticks and barking like dogs and whooping it up in general. The idea was to make enough noise to scare the boars out of the feeding area.

Finally I heard something coming through the underbrush from the general direction of the brush beaters. Then I saw six wild boars running in and slightly above the deer run. The first hunter cut loose at the leader with his .30/06 autoloading rifle. He scored with his fifth shot. The 200-pound boar went down for keeps without a squeal.

It was now my turn. I was shooting a new .44 Magnum autoloading carbine built for brush-country shooting. I picked out the tusker that appeared to have the best head for mounting (as nearly as I could tell, two of the boars were females) and eased off my first shot, which was a miss. I saw bark fly off the body of a bush almost a foot over the tusker. It is very easy to misjudge while shooting down a mountainside like that. The boar was not traveling too fast, but fast enough to make him a tough target in brush country like this. I lowered my sighting

The boar was about to charge the hunter when this photo was made. A wounded or cornered boar can be dangerous if he gets a chance to use his wicked tusks. (*Tennessee Game and Fish Commission photo*)

point on the next shot, doing my best to hold on the boar's front feet, and let go with another 240-grain soft-nosed bullet. The boar did a half somersault and went down for keeps.

The next stander got a good shot at a big 250-pound boar that had been too much in the underbrush above the deer run for me to get a good shot at. He was shooting a .308-caliber autoloader, and his first shot put the big tusker down. The boar started letting out hair-raising squeals as soon as he hit the ground, however, and this almost always spells trouble if other boars happen to be near. When one of their number starts squealing in agony, other boars near the spot will almost invariably come "whooshing" in to the rescue and charge any creature in sight.

The excited hunter sent a second slug into the dying boar to finish him off quickly and stop the squealing, but even so the action was too late to stop a charge from one of the other boars. I was easing in from the rear to help him out if necessary (our stands were about seventy-five yards apart) and saw him cut the boar down as the angry beast charged up the mountain toward him. The two females then cut back across the top of the mountain and disappeared.

The experience just described points out two more important things about wild-boar hunting. A boar shot down but still able to squeal may bring danger from other tuskers in a hurry. Where dogs are being used such rarely happens, but on the driver-stander hunts, hunters should be on the alert for this possible danger.

This experience also describes another type of boar hunting. This system can be used both on and off the preserves with equal results. Which system gives the average hunter the best chance to bag a wild boar depends on several things.

I personally have had better results on hunts where the latter system was employed. Others I know have had better success on the dog hunts. Where several (six to twelve) boars are feeding in a small area, the noisy drives are probably the best method. Where the tuskers are scattered out more and feeding over a wider area, the dog-hunt system is probably the best way.

A few have tried wild-boar hunting with bow and arrow. Take a tip and don't. The critters are too tough to stop for archery tackle as a general rule. I was on one hunt in Tennessee's Tellico area a few years back when it took fourteen shots to bring a 325-pound boar down for keeps.

Here's an example of how tough a boar can be. The natives called this special boar "Old Hitler." The grizzled old tusker had whipped every boar pack to a frazzle, but finally one day a party of hunters with their dogs got the old boy cornered in a deep canyon called Jeffrey's Hell. At least five hunters got shots at Old Hitler with .30/30s, .30/06s, and .35s, and when the mad old tusker finally went down he had been hit by thirteen high-powered rifle slugs in non-vital places. A 12-gauge rifled slug in the spine was the blow that finally made the kill. This tough old boar was knocked down three times before the 12-gauge slug finally got him, but each time he got up and tried to escape. Old Hitler killed three boar dogs during this fight for his life and seriously wounded two others. He also knocked down two hunters during the hair-raising ten minutes, and sent a photographer skinning up a tree like a gray squirrel.

We now come to the important point of guns and loads for boar hunting. An elephant gun is not necessary, and a varmint rifle certainly not advisable. The best boar-hunting combination lies somewhere in between these two extremes.

Practically all wild-boar hunting in the United States is done in brush country where the flat-trajectory "phoom" calibers are not advisable. A bullet that will blow up on contact with average undergrowth is out as a boar load because a good share of the shots at these animals will be in dense undergrowth areas.

As already indicated, the wild boar is a hard animal to stop unless it is hit vitally. A bullet or slug with a lot of quick knockdown wallop is the best and safest bet, and it should be a bullet or slug that will plow through average underbrush with a good reasonable degree of accuracy.

A lot of experienced boar hunters are using the newer 12-gauge pump and autoloading shotguns designed especially for shooting rifled slug loads. They prefer the shorter models over the longer ones. In other words, the shorter barreled models.

Shooting modern rifled slug loads, these guns are truly deadly on boar and most other big game up to a distance of sixty yards

235

in brush country. Within this range the combination has terrific knockdown power, and is sufficiently accurate for this type of hunting.

I have tried them both, and I personally prefer the .44 Magnum carbine-type autoloader over all other guns for boar hunting. This rifle, using factory ammo, holds good accuracy up to 125 yards, and also has terrific knockdown power (or wallop) anywhere within this range.

My own third choice would be a .30/06 in the newer and shorter brush-shooting type (pump or autoloader), and for boar 220-grain soft-point bullets. For those who still prefer the old, reliable lever-action carbines, the newer and shorter brush-country models in .30/30 caliber, using 150-grain soft-point bullets, will do the job. The shorter rifles and shotguns are a lot handier to get around in the brush if quick action becomes necessary, and guns capable of long-range kills are not necessary in boar hunting.

Equip the boar gun with a carrying sling, but forget about scope sights and all other extras. No one needs a scoped rifle for boar hunting. Imagine trying to place the cross hairs of a scope on a charging boar in territory where the underbrush is thick!

Some of the boar hunting in southeastern United States is of the managed-hunt variety. Most of the dog hunts in the wildlife-management areas (other hunts, too, as for that matter) are managed hunts. Parties, however, may number up to a hundred hunters, and every year hunters from all parts of the nation come in to enjoy this unique sport.

The boar-hunting preserves have six-month seasons, and kills are guaranteed. The guides will stick with a guest until he gets his boar. It is the surest way to get a boar, and the hunting is just as real and wild and rugged as it is on the vast wildlife-management areas and other mountain territories.

Just remember this—when you tackle wild boars, be on the alert, because the critters are as unpredictable as the wind.

In the southeast there is another type of wild hog that roams parts of Florida, Georgia, Louisiana, Mississippi, Arkansas, Tennessee, and North Carolina. These wild swine are as wild and vicious as the exotic wild boars and may be found in vast swamp jungles or up in the mountains.

They are domestic hogs that have been on their own in wilderness areas so long that they have reverted to the wild. They no longer closely resemble their barnyard cousins. They are called, depending on the territory they are found in, "razorbacks," "ridge runners," "sharpshooters," and "acorn splitters." They are long-snouted, beady-eyed, flop-eared, vile-tempered, and often wickedly tusked.

In some of the jungly swamp sections of Florida the wild razorbacks are hunted with dogs and actually hog-tied with ropes at the end of the chase. Hunters follow the dogs on horseback, and at least one in the party will carry a .357 Magnum handgun just in case the razorback is too vicious to hog-tie. Otherwise someone tosses a loop around the bayed critter's neck, another loop around a hind leg, and from there on the hog-tying operation is a thrilling, grueling, and sometimes even hazardous job. This is certainly no sport for coffee-bar hunters and armchair sports.

238   Howard Sigler.

Chapter Twenty

BOW HUNTING TIPS
by HOWARD SIGLER

HOWARD SIGLER is a rural mail carrier who covers about forty miles daily on his mail route in the vicinity of Harrisville, West Virginia, where he lives. This job takes a half day, so it leaves his afternoons free for hunting, fishing, exploration, and writing. He has hunted with guns since boyhood and didn't take up archery or bow hunting until 1955. But since then he has become highly skilled in this challenging sport and is now recognized as an authority in this field. He writes a monthly column in *Tam—The Archers' Magazine* and is Archery Editor for *Leisure,* the exclusive magazine for customer reading in barber shops. He also writes weekly outdoor columns for newspapers and articles for the outdoor magazines. He is author of *The Pocket Field Guide to Archery.*

ANYWHERE hunting tales are being swapped, "luck" pops up sooner or later, and bowhunters are more susceptible to the term than any other group. Some go so far as to credit 75 per cent of bow hunting success to luck; others place it even higher, and the writer wholeheartedly agrees that it does play a big part in every hunt.

However, did you ever notice that the luckiest hunters are usually those who conscientiously work at it harder, always looking for new kinks, trying to learn more about game habits, all ears when the experienced or tyros come up with a new tale or idea? From that slant, let's see if we can't find a few ways to give our luck a boost.

Just before sunset one evening, I was heading homeward through the shadows just below the crest of a hilltop field when I saw a good whitetailed buck coming toward me, but angling toward the skyline. I froze instantly, and, as I was well camouflaged and had the shadows as background, he didn't see me but continued on out of sight over the hilltop. The rut was on, and

I knew that if he heard any unusual sound he would come back for a look-see, so I hotfooted it toward the crest, making some noise and trying to get as close under him as possible before he reappeared. Things happened more quickly than I had anticipated. When I had covered only half of the sixty-odd yards, I saw antlers tip the skyline, and I froze in mid-stride—but *unluckily* with my right foot uphill and well forward. As any right-handed archer knows, in that position it is next to impossible to shoot straight ahead or even a *little* to the right, so there I was! Only thirty yards away, the deer quickly came into complete broadside silhouette against the sunset, headed toward my right. He looked in my direction but apparently could not quite pin-point me, so he just stopped and looked. Attempting to move my foot, I found the grass too dry and noisy, so for long minutes we remained in our respective positions, with me helpless as a babe. Finally, he gave his antlers a toss and whirled back over the ridge to become lost in the sundown thickets—and I felt like an idiot!

Meeting the deer *was* happenstance or luck, but getting caught unprepared for a shot was certainly not unlucky—it was plain poor management. That type of "bad luck" never caught me again. When making any stalk, particularly uphill, where it may be necessary to shoot quickly to the right, I step with my left foot, then bring my right up *to,* but not past it. With the feet placed with the left forward or even side by side, one can, by pivoting at the hips, shoot at practically any tangent within a 270° arc, the blank spot being that area behind the right shoulder. Conditions are reversed, of course, for left-handed shooters.

While we are on the subject of feet and footwork, let me say that sturdy but lightweight, well-fitting hunting boots are a must for the bow hunter. No clodhoppers in this business. In my own hill country, the heel-type is preferable to those with the wedge sole, for they will save many a tumble. Nothing is more discouraging (unlucky?) than to have a foot go out from under you on a downhill bed of dry-slick leaves just as one nears the end of a tedious, perfect up-to-then stalk.

The hunter must become accustomed to his footwear and have it completely broken in far in advance of actual hunting use, whether it be for deer, predator calling, or chucking the summer meadows. Once the shoes become a part of your feet, no matter what type rubber sole, you can "feel out" sticks and uneven ground without actually looking down except for an occasional glance to lay your course.

In all bow hunting, other than straight woods-walking to cover ground, the hunter should correlate his steps with body balance, so that he may stop at any instant, in whatever portion of his step necessity finds him. If one foot has just left the ground, be able to keep it in mid-air until whatever sound you hear is identified or until you can carefully place that foot back in the print it just left. This is especially important when hunting in dry woods where bare or noiseless spots are at a premium.

Ordinarily, animals will be making as much noise in the autumn woods as you, if you travel fairly quietly, so by timing your steps and being prepared to stop instantly, it is often possible to hear them before they do you. An old still-hunting rule of thumb is to take one step and wait two, then pause for a few minutes about every fifty feet and scan the area ahead thoroughly. Never top a rise without scanning the other side *at your eye level*. Just barely peep over. When deer hunting, watch your back trail as well.

Since the bow hunter cannot "jump shoot" deer to any advantage (and neither can most gunners), he must travel through the woods and coverts so as to attract the minimum of attention. Only one place is this possible, other than on man-made woods roads and paths—and that is on the deer trails themselves.

Deer expect travel on their highways, particularly during the rut when bucks are roaming at all hours of the day and night, so if the hunter goes carefully and makes like a deer as much as he can, he has a great advantage.

Look at it this way. In your home town you pay little attention to people walking on the sidewalks, yet let someone start across the back yards and everyone in the neighborhood will be looking to see what's going on. The same thing works in the woods. All animals expect travel along the game trails.

Frequently the fall woods are so dry that walking, even semi-noiselessly, is impractical. Under such conditions it is better to do your hunting from a stand or blind. Clear off the leaves down to bare ground so that you may move your feet quietly, get put, and *stay there*. This is the most monotonous yet the most efficiently deadly method of bow hunting deer. It hasn't the glamour or thrill of the still hunt or stalk, but if the hunter situates himself properly near the downwind of a much-used crossing or trail and sticks it out for a few successive mornings and evenings, it is almost sure fire for success, if he can shoot worth a hoot.

When it is necessary to woods-walk or you wish to still-hunt under dry conditions, it is best to try to imitate the sounds of leaf travel of deer, squirrels, or other woods creatures. A man walking through leaves sounds like nothing else in the woods, but by moving hesitantly, and with a minimum of leaf-crunching (no snapping of sticks!), he may disguise his travel sounds with sometimes amazing results in almost plain view of his quarry.

In recent years the deer hunter has taken to the trees, and his kill percentage has gone up as well. Being off the ground has many advantages which outweigh the disadvantages considerably. In the first place, for some reason deer do not often look up. They know the ground of their home area as we do our back yard and can spot anything strange in a jiffy, either giving the suspected danger point nervous but intent scrutiny or immediately spooking. At the same time, they pay little attention to what is above them. I have been in plain view a mere six feet off the ground and had deer walk complacently under me.

Under most conditions, the hunter's scent is carried off into the upper air, thus giving the tree stand a tremendous advantage over the ground blind. Winds may shift, which on the ground might immediately be fatal to the whole setup, but in a tree it makes little difference. Also, the hunter is up where he can see over the undergrowth and know what is going on far beyond his immediate area. One of my favorite stands is built some ten feet off the ground in a small patch of woods, practically surrounded by old, overgrown fields, and with binocs, I can see everything going on for over five hundred yards in the entire downhill area. You may watch your game coming long before it gets within range—and range from a tree stand can be right down to five or ten yards!

On the ground, the trail watcher must remain practically motionless for long periods, whereas in the tree some movement is permissible. You can't go into a dance, but you may move around to keep warm, scan the area with binoculars at your leisure, and generally not have to make like a statue. It *is* better, however, to have a convenient place to hang your bow (with an arrow on the string) so it and its flashy bow quiver won't be moving each time you do. With your long-look, there will usually be ample time to get it. Keep the hands still except for slow movements. Put them in your pockets if they want to fidget.

What is considered the chief disadvantage to this type of hunting is one's inability to move from one location to another readily. The remedy is to study your area thoroughly and be sure your location is where it will do the most good. I like mine, ·if practicable, to be about ten yards uphill or downwind (if in flat country) from a well-traveled main trail. Then the stand works *for* you. It is there, it cannot move, and neither can you— so you cannot decide, right in the middle of things, that "just over there" would be a better place. Locate it properly, stick with it, and don't lose faith just because deer don't show up the first time. Before you know it, you'll have more deer within spitting distance than you ever saw in all your ground-hunting days.

Make these stands in advance of the season if it is at all possible, and, at the same time, lay yourself a trail so you may reach it easily and quietly before daylight and leave in the same manner after an evening hunt. Be sure there is a convenient snag to hang your bow and binocs; if there isn't, use a nail. Also have one on which to hang your bow while mounting the stand, for you cannot climb quietly and carry a bow too. If limbs are not convenient for climbing, I nail cleats to the tree sides or, if the stand is built between two trees, nail pieces of saplings between them like ladder rungs. In the construction, don't leave evidence of a big operation around the tree. Work carefully, and keep things looking natural.

Portable tree stands are on the market which are quite sturdy

When hunting open fields, stay low and keep your silhouette below the horizon. The human form should never appear against the skyline.

and easy to put up and which take the cut-and-dried permanency out of the location. Mine is of Polar brand and never even creaks under my two hundred pounds. It goes up in mid-October and stays one place or another in the woods until January. After three years of such use (plus summertime wildlife observation, etc.) it is still in good shape. A heavy chain secures it to the tree, and it may be padlocked to prevent theft.

Whether it's summertime woodchucking, bowfishing for big carp along the rivers, flu-fluing for squirrels among the hardwoods, or prowling the deer thickets of autumn and deep winter, the bow-hunter's clothing must not only be soft, quiet material but must also blend in with the outdoor background, or none of the tricks will work. I admit that deer and many other animals are color-blind to an extent and a red wool shirt will work just as well on them as Kamo cloth, but when one is seeking them that doesn't eliminate other creatures in the same territory. To name a few, crows, hawks, jays, squirrels (both ground and tree) and foxes are all apparently able to distinguish color as we know it, while grouse are even capable of separating the camouflaged human form from a blending background. To disturb or alarm any of these, can easily set off a woodland chain reaction that will not only tell your whitetail quarry that danger is in the neighborhood but may practically pinpoint it; upon which, if they are curious enough, they will circle downwind to satisfy themselves; then the jig is up. I frequently shoot squirrels which approach me while on a deer stand before they can give the alarm, risking the sound of the muffled bowstring in preference to their far-reaching chatter.

Soft wool, poplin, and similar materials are best and may be of practically any subdued shade if one doesn't want to go in for regular camouflage. Hunting shirts of plain or mottled pattern are preferable to solid colors, but stay away from the whites and yellows in color combinations. These colors offer *contrast*, and that is where the danger lies. Bright yellow and the fluorescent shades of all other colors should be avoided because of their greater contrast. The advantage of five-shade green-brown Kamo clothing is not so much in its color as in its blending, mottled effect.

245

A very efficient camouflage shirt may be doped up at home, a tan cotton work shirt of sufficient size to go over other clothing being ideal for this purpose. First, use dark brown shoe dye and splotch it up in any way that suits your fancy. Let this dry, then give it a heavy tinting with dark green Rit. A complete dye job isn't necessary, for tinting works just as well if very hot water is used and the shirt is left in a sufficient time. Give it plenty of cold rinsing afterward, until the water comes out clear, and add a good dose of salt to one of the final ones to set the color. I still occasionally use one of these I made up years ago.

Above all, when you wear the shirt collar open, do not wear white undershirts. White is, generally speaking, an unnatural color to the woods, and that small patch at the neck may easily render the rest of your camouflage useless. My hunting T-shirts are all tinted dark green or brown. The same goes for a white handkerchief. During gunning season this is also an invitation to get shot by some tyro hunter, who is accustomed only to seeing the white tails of deer as they skedaddle away through the thickets.

When snow predominates on the hunting scene, a white parka is a real asset. Since any parka's head covering obstructs efficient hearing, fold it down inside the back and wear a white knit cap instead. You must hunt with your ears as well as your eyes (and frequently, nose), so they should never be covered unless it is really necessary; then it is usually too cold for much game to be stirring anyway. White trousers are fine but not necessary. By experience, it seems to me that most wildlife apparently considers anything seen moving near the ground simply another creature, so wearing the white camouflage above is usually sufficient. Nor is it necessary to color the bow or equip it with a white bow sock. It will appear to be just another sapling or tree limb at a little distance. Use your regular autumn bow camouflage.

While the sound of a plain bowstring will spook most wildlife, both because of the "twang" and high-frequency vibrations created, the "thud" of a well-muffled one does not carry far at all, nor does it particularly disturb game when a miss is made.

Though not as roomy as homemade ones, portable tree stands suit the bow-hunter's needs admirably. Since they may be attached to any medium-sized tree, they are adaptable to almost any area or trail situation.

This past season, two large bucks were in the vicinity of one of my tree stands, and, as is the common tendency when shooting from a height, I overshot the nearer one. He only snorted and scooted into the nearby underbrush, where he fooled around, snorting occasionally, for perhaps a half hour before departing. The other, about a hundred yards distant, did not even move until many minutes later when other business (does) beckoned from the opposite hillside.

Strings may be muffled by tying large rubber bands midway between each tip and the served center portion. Several kinds of inexpensive gadgets for this purpose are on the market, however, and they do the job better and longer. I use double sets on

The plastic lure cartridge is opened and carried on the belt, letting its scent drift with the wind to cover human odor.

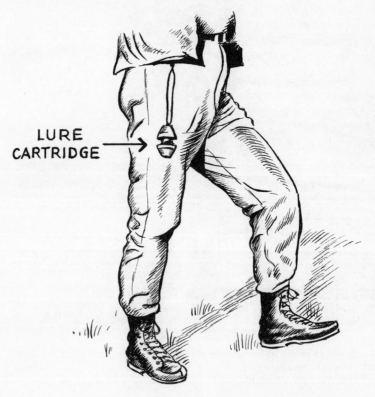

LURE
CARTRIDGE

my hunting bows, two being placed equidistant from each other, between tip and nocking point, on each end of the string. Such arrangement does not hinder the bow's cast in the least.

As all archers are aware, the arrow must be released from the same place on the bowstring each time, and a *shooting knot* or *nocking point* is placed there as a guide. For finger protection, a shooting glove or tab is worn on that hand. In hunting and bowfishing, this glove becomes a nuisance in many ways, so a few years ago I did away with this item. Instead, I employ the No-Glov bowstring attachment, made of molded rubber in two sections. It is slipped over the loop and down the string to the desired position. The hunter shoots bare-handed or, in cold weather, may wear buckskin gloves.

Hunting requires practice, just as does tournament shooting, but, in my book, hunting practice is of greater importance. The difference between clean-killing or cruelly wounding a wild animal is at stake, and it is up to you, the hunter, which it will be. My own rule for practice is to never use regulation circular targets. Life-size ones, yes—but here the second part of my rule comes in. Never take two successive shots from the same place, distance, or position. One rarely gets "setups" in the woods, so practice should approach the hunting situation as closely as possible. I prefer to shoot at leaves, clumps of grass, sticks, and the like at any and all distances, with woodchuck and other small-game and varmint hunting the prelude to deer season. If you intend to use tree stands, take plenty of practice shooting from a height. To repeat, the tendency here is to overshoot.

Scent or "lure" can either work for or against you. If the hunter's body and clothing are clean and free from odor foreign to the woodlands, scent may be used to advantage, but there isn't a so-called lure made which will fool a deer if it is mixed with either plain "unwashed" odor—or shaving lotion. The best cover-up scent of all is plain skunk essence, for it is natural to the outdoors. I use it in a gadget called the Miracle-Lure cartridge, made of plastic with a felt wick inside. Of screw-closure type, it may be carried safely in the pocket. In its open state, it may be hung from the belt, letting the skunk scent drift where it may. It will cover up, never fear, and is, besides, rather attractive to deer. These cartridges ordinarily come filled with a fine deer lure, but may be purchased with an untreated wick to which the skunk smell is applied.

Another kink is to put the stuff on a small square of wool sheepskin and fasten it to your upper bow limb with a rubber band. This, of course, necessitates a new piece of wool every time out, for you don't take that stuff into the house.

No matter what I am hunting, some kind of scent is on my person, if not in a cartridge, then on my feet to disguise my trail. A small piece of woolskin or heavy felt is sewn to a loop of elastic so it will fit snugly around my ankle, about halfway forward so it will rub against the grasses as I walk. One ankle is sufficient. On the pad goes a few drops of scent. For woodchucking I use either chuck or rabbit; skunk or rabbit for predator calling or hunting; and for deer, I use deer lure made from the glands of a doe in heat. Where there is no grass, turn the pad underneath, just in front of the heel, so a trail will be left on the ground. The last buck killed with a rifle had his nose to the ground trailing me like a beagle hot on a rabbit track.

On every hunt, both a predator call and hawk call will be in my pocket. The former will often bring woodchucks out of their dens, roving foxes in from across the valley, crows from as far as they can hear it, and rabbits out of brier patches in nothing flat.

The hawk call does not call hawks—it is a "freezing" call. One squeal and a too-frisky squirrel will flatten against a limb, ready-to-fly grouse will wait just a little longer, and already-called-in foxes may be stopped just about where you want them for a shot.

Similarly, unless they are spooked by actual danger, a low "Baa-a-a!" like a sheep (or deer) will cause four out of five moving deer to hesitate long enough for a shot, this being particularly applicable to bucks during the rut. Upon one occasion, though too far for a shot, I made a buck stop and turn five times before he went out of sight.

Finally, keep yourself in top hunting condition mentally. The psychological approach to hunting is calm, cold, deadly relaxation. Figure what you're going to do and do it, easy and without bumbling around. When you draw, don't *wonder if* you will make a hit—*know* it's going to be there. Many times it won't, but never let that shake your confidence in yourself. That shot is past history, you'll make the next one! To retain this psychological level, never attempt a shot that you know is impossible beforehand. Better let the game slip quietly away for a better chance some other time. As sportsman bow hunters, our aim is to kill cleanly. Learn to shoot properly, know your limitations, stay within them—and keep your broadheads sharp!